Core Practices for Project-Based Learning

Core Practices in Education

Series edited by Pam Grossman

OTHER BOOKS IN THIS SERIES

*Preparing Science Teachers
Through Practice-Based Teacher Education*
Edited by David Stroupe,
Karen Hammerness, and Scott McDonald

*Teaching Core Practices
in Teacher Education*
Edited by Pam Grossman

Core Practices for Project-Based Learning

A GUIDE FOR
TEACHERS AND LEADERS

Pam Grossman

Zachary Herrmann

Sarah Schneider Kavanagh

Christopher G. Pupik Dean

HARVARD EDUCATION PRESS
Cambridge, Massachusetts

Paperback ISBN 978-1-68253-642-1
Library Edition ISBN 978-1-68253-643-8

Library of Congress Cataloging-in-Publication data is on file.

Published by Harvard Education Press,
an imprint of the Harvard Education Publishing Group

Harvard Education Press
8 Story Street
Cambridge, MA 02138

Cover Design: Ciano Design
Cover Photo: Lora Reehling Photography

The typefaces used in this book are Hermann and Monterchi.

— CONTENTS —

ONE

Core Practices of
Project-Based Learning

I t's Tuesday morning and there are thirty-two students grouped around eight tables in Ms. Johnson's twelfth-grade government class. At any given moment, you can hear at least fifteen different voices in the air as the students at each table negotiate their work with one another—some with raised voices and some in quiet conversation. The class is two weeks' deep into working on a project that has them examining how different branches of government work together to implement public policy. Rather than have students sit and listen to lectures on this topic, Ms. Johnson has built partnerships with four interest groups around the city that have each agreed to review student-generated political action plans that further their policy agenda: a neighborhood alliance, a non-profit associated with the local watershed, a public health organization, and the town's historical society. (In her first year of doing this project with students, she had only one partner, but over the past six years of doing this project with her seniors, it's grown to be much bigger than she first imagined it could be.) Creating these political action plans, Ms. Johnson is hoping, will support students to learn about how congressional committees and the bureaucracy work together with interest groups to create public policy. All of Ms. Johnson's grand hopes and big plans have resulted in a classroom that is loud and busy and, to an outsider, completely confusing.

Every group seems to be doing something different. One group of four girls has sequestered themselves into the far corner of the classroom, and they are barely speaking with one another. Each of them has on headphones as they type out drafts of the different action plan sections that they've assigned themselves. To their left is a group in which it seems like every member is speaking at once as they debate some basic principles of their plan. Across the room, Ms. Johnson is crouched down with a group that has struggled to schedule their interviews with key members of the interest group they chose—a requirement of the project. As they regale her with the drama of their scheduling woes, she asks them what they can determine from the interest group's website and supplementary documents because they don't yet have interviews to fall back on. As she's engaged in this gentle prodding, she is also half-listening to a debate going on in the group to her right about the phrases "issue network" and "iron triangle," concepts they have gone over in previous classes and that are central to understanding policy-making but, as she can half-hear in her eavesdropping, are still not clear to some students.

This classroom is full of authentic, meaningful activity. It is a classroom ripe with opportunities to learn. It is also, however, a classroom where things could easily go wrong—and fast. To harness all the energy and possibility hanging in the air, Ms. Johnson must be able to set up productive collaborations and respond in the moment. She needs to know how to get the four girls in the corner to collaborate with one another so that their action plan doesn't read like four disconnected research papers. She needs to know how to check in with the entire class about the concepts of issue networks and the iron triangle to see if these concepts are confusing to everyone or just a select few. After she has determined what to do, she needs to find a way to build students' understanding without abandoning the project in favor of a lecture. In addition, she needs a way to track each group's progress toward the project's intended outcomes so that no group falls through the (seemingly many) cracks of this loud and busy classroom. On top of all of this, she needs to manage her outside partnerships and know enough about policy-making herself to recognize when her students are stumbling upon a critical idea and when they're stumbling into a rabbit hole of misconceptions. This kind of teaching is not for the faint of heart. Its complexity can make it feel overwhelming and intimidating. It is no wonder that we so rarely see this approach to teaching and learning in classrooms around the country; in fact, we might begin to wonder—*how would a teacher even begin to learn to do this well?*

This question has undergirded our work at the University of Pennsylvania Project-Based Learning Certificate Program. In pursuit of answers to this question, we have conducted research and worked with hundreds of teachers, educational leaders, and curriculum designers working in contexts all over the country and, increasingly, around the world. Through our work, we have met many inspiring educators, some who are deeply experienced in project-based learning (or PBL) and some who are just getting started, but all of whom were courageous in the face of a daunting task: turning their classrooms into places where students engage in meaningful, authentic activity that makes a real contribution to the world.

DEFINING PROJECT-BASED LEARNING

Before we explore how the teachers we've worked with learned to facilitate meaningful project-based learning, it might be helpful to pause to make sure we have a shared understanding of what such learning looks like. While project-based learning has no single, precise definition, its advocates generally agree on certain basic characteristics of the approach.[1] These features include identifying a project or problem that students work on (often with peers), engaging in sustained inquiry, getting feedback and critique that supports revision, sharing the work with a wider audience, and then reflecting on the learning that happened across the process.

Although practitioners and scholars may conceptualize these elements in somewhat different ways, all of them incorporate most of these components in their project-based practice.

As numerous commentators have noted, these approaches are not new but are firmly rooted in the progressive era and recurring efforts to engage students more actively in their learning. The current enthusiasm for project-based learning may reflect the fact that this pedagogical approach is particularly well matched to the ambitious twenty-first century learning goals of collaboration, creativity, communication, critical thinking, and flexible uses of technology. As more and more jobs require teamwork and collaboration, often remotely, project-based learning can provide an opportunity to develop these capacities alongside the cultivation of more traditional academic goals, including content knowledge and the development of academic skills.

Project-based learning can take many forms when it is enacted in schools. In some cases, the entire curriculum is project-based, with projects serving as the curricular glue for student learning. At the Workshop School in Philadelphia, for example, all freshmen work on a project to rehab a food truck and develop a healthy menu of foods to sell. Through the project, they learn about auto mechanics, science, nutrition, business, and communication skills, as well as develop the ability to collaborate as part of a team. However, in many instances, projects comprise part of a larger curriculum that also incorporates other, non-project-based activities for student learning. For example, in an English language arts (ELA) class, a project designed to have students write and produce a play around a social issue of their choosing might sit alongside writing workshops and discussions of literary texts. In a geometry class, for example, a group project that requires students to design and construct a giant inflatable geometric solid using a plastic table cloth and packing tape might also include other instructional activities including mini-lessons on geometric nets and flat patterns, problem sets requiring students to calculate the surface area for a variety of geometric forms, and small group activities where students produce and analyze small paper models.

Similarly, the contexts in which teachers engage students in PBL also differ. Schools like High Tech High or The Workshop School identify themselves as project-based schools where all teachers and students are engaged in project-based teaching and learning. In these schools, teachers have easy access to colleagues who share a similar instructional approach. Their students are in other classes in which they are also engaged in projects, so the skills developed in one class support the work in another. In establishing norms for collaboration or critique, these teachers often do not have to start from scratch. Such schools, while still the exception, are growing in number. EL Education (formally known as Expeditionary Learning) has long championed an experiential, project-based approach and has grown to a network of schools. Many of the XQ schools funded by the Emerson Collective have featured different approaches to project-based and experiential learning as well.

There are other signs that the PBL approach is growing in popularity. At the district level, Chicago Public Schools now require that all students engage in a service-learning project. Massachusetts recently enacted a law that requires all public secondary schools in the state to provide opportunities for all students to engage in student-led civics projects that are designed to help students analyze complex issues, consider different perspectives, engage in civil discourse, and learn more about the functioning of local, state, and federal governments.[2] These efforts will require school leaders to consider ways of supporting project-based work for large numbers of teachers and students. Why? Because projects don't teach themselves, and most teachers rightfully find project-based teaching far more complex than more traditional forms of teaching, often requiring additional support and professional learning. Other teachers, however, work in schools in which they might be one of only a very few teachers who are experimenting with PBL. In fact, given what we know about the current state of teaching and learning, this is likely to be the norm. Even with the support of administrators, teachers in these contexts might feel as though they are "swimming against the tide," in asking their students to engage with a fundamentally different way of "doing school."

BECOMING A PBL TEACHER

In our work, we have come across teachers working in a variety of contexts. Some were introduced to PBL by the administration at their schools, whereas others felt that they were on their own, enacting PBL despite a lack of support from their school or district. Regardless of the context, however, each one of the teachers that we've worked with and learned from had, at some point along the way, committed to the slow and steady process of transforming their practice. The work that we present in this book comes from a long-term examination of these teachers' experiences as they've grown into their PBL practice. Our studies have revealed to us important insights about how teachers can learn to engage in authentic, student-centered, active learning pedagogies.

As we listened to teachers talk about how they transformed their practice, we were struck by how frequently certain themes came up. Teachers who learned to do this work well often weren't trying to transform everything at once. They understood that they couldn't change all aspects of their instruction overnight. They worked slowly and steadily to change one thing at a time and had clear goals for themselves that they worked toward. They had ways to get feedback on their progress toward these goals from other teachers in their social networks, and they had visions of what learning would look like in their classroom if they achieved these goals. The revolutions in their practice were not overnight overthrows of the tyranny of the lecture. They were small, thoughtful, incremental, goal-directed changes, which resulted over time in radical instructional change.

While this incremental approach to teacher learning aligns with our common sense and most people's experiences in learning anything new, it requires something that most of us don't have when it comes to authentic, student-centered, active learning pedagogies: a clear place to start and then clear next steps that are manageable and concrete. Most people, even many of the experts we've encountered in our years investigating how teachers learn to enact project-based learning, have a more holistic perspective. Again and again, we've heard people say that when it comes to meaningful project-based learning, they "know it when they see it." While this perspective might help someone *hire* talented teachers, it does little to help teachers *learn* to transform their practice. If *"I know it when I see it"* could help people learn something new, anyone who has seen Serena Williams play tennis would be a competitor at Wimbledon. A vision of the whole is necessary, but without a deep understanding of the parts that make up that whole, learning is impossible. If we acknowledge that authentic, active learning pedagogies take time and effort for teachers to learn, then we must develop a vision of all the small instructional components that make up the whole of a practice that puts students at the center of their own learning.

In pursuit of understanding the parts that make up the whole of student-centered, active learning, we have spent years studying expert practitioners in project-based learning. Our goal was to better understand their instructional practice so that we might help teachers who are newer to this work follow in their footsteps. From what we learned from these experts, we now run a certificate program for teachers who want to become skilled at project-based learning, and throughout this book, you'll hear stories inspired by the experiences of the hundreds of teachers who have participated in this program. Like this book, the program is grounded in a framework of core practices of project-based learning that was developed out of our research. To understand where our ideas have come from, we want to give you a brief overview of the research undergirding what you are about to read.

OUR RESEARCH INTO PBL TEACHERS' PRACTICE

Determined to be able to describe meaningful, student-centered, active learning pedagogy in more detail than "I know it when I see it," we embarked on a study in 2015 that brought us into classrooms and into conversations with accomplished PBL teachers as well as those eager to develop their PBL practice, inspiring principals of PBL schools, and dedicated educational leaders working in organizations that promote project-based learning. What we learned from these teachers and leaders has transformed the work we do with educators at the University of Pennsylvania. We began our research by surveying experts in PBL and asking them what they saw as the key features of high-quality PBL classrooms. We followed our surveys with interviews of accomplished PBL teachers and then collected videos of their classroom practice. Looking across these data, we found that the teachers focused on four primary goals: supporting deep *disciplinary* content learning, engaging students in *authentic* work, supporting student *collaboration*, and building an *iterative* culture where students are always prototyping, reflecting, redesigning, editing, and trying again. To achieve these goals, the teachers enacted a repertoire of teaching practices. We have come to call these the *core practices of project-based teaching* (see figure 1.1).

WHY ORGANIZE AROUND CORE PRACTICES?

Our decision to organize our framework around a set of core practices of teaching is a choice that was born out of our previous work and the work of a number of other teacher educators and researchers. We've chosen to focus on teaching practice as a lever of educational change because we see teachers themselves as the most important players in any effort to radically transform education. All other levers—policies, structures, curricula, professional development—have to move through teachers before they reach students. Our belief is that when we take the practice of teachers seriously, when we treat teachers as the most important piece of the puzzle, we're much more likely to effect meaningful educational change for students. And working toward this kind of radical transformation is important. For decades there has been a stubborn persistence of approaches to teaching that maintain the educational status quo and ensure that classrooms remain places where teachers talk and students listen. And disappointingly, but perhaps unsurprisingly, the students who are most likely to be subjected to rote and decontextualized instruction are students of color and students living in poverty. Our hope is that by offering teachers and leaders approaches to transforming teaching practices, we might interrupt the educational status quo and offer students who have been consistently denied access to meaningful and authentic activity in classrooms a new

FIGURE 1.1   Full framework

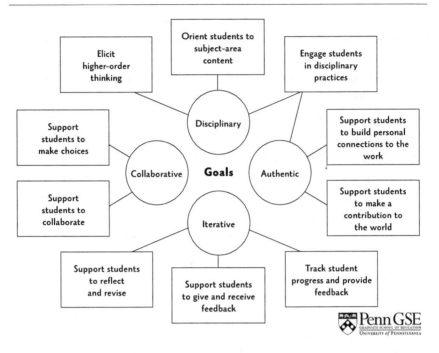

Source: Pam Grossman, Christopher Pupik Dean, Sarah Schneider Kavanagh, and Zachary Herrmann. "Preparing Teachers for Project-Based Teaching." kappanonline.org, March 25, 2019. https://kappanonline.org/preparing-teachers-project-based-teaching-grossman-pupik-dean-kavanagh-herrmann/.

educational reality—one that puts them, their ideas, their passions, and their potential at the center.

Our work is only one part of a larger effort to move opportunities for teacher learning closer to actual teacher practice. Both teacher education and professional development in this country have been accused of being too theoretical, focusing on idealized theories rather than the gritty realities of classroom practice. Practice-based teacher education tries to infuse examples of practice in a wide variety of forms—including classroom videos and student work—and create more opportunities for teachers to try out different approaches to teaching in the context of university classrooms and professional development spaces. For example, in learning how to lead rich, student-centered discussions in their classrooms, novice teachers might watch videos of more experienced teachers engaging their students in a discussion and then try out different ways to get students to build on each other's ideas.

One element of a practice-based approach to teacher development consists of identifying a set of foundational practices that teachers might need to be successful and then creating opportunities for teachers to develop those practices. As we outline in a companion volume, these practices provide the fulcrum for professional learning opportunities that range from careful analysis of the practices through video examples and live observation to enactment of the practices in the context of both professional education settings and K–12 classrooms.[3] In some efforts, including those by TeachingWorks at the University of Michigan, teacher educators work on practices that cut across content areas, which they term high leverage practices, including communicating with parents, leading a group discussion, and implementing norms and routines for classroom discourse and work.[4] Other groups have focused on more subject-specific practices, such as practices for teaching historical inquiry or science.[5] Our goal in this book is geared around identifying a set of practices that help support teachers in enacting a particular instructional approach—project-based learning— across grade levels and content areas, with the hope that we could support teachers in ensuring that all students have opportunities to benefit from project-based learning, particularly those students who, because of their family's income, their race, or their zip code, have all too often been denied opportunities to exercise agency and ownership for their learning.

Our framework of core practices for PBL is organized around instructional goals—what teachers hope to achieve through a project-based approach. When a teacher decides to enact a practice in a particular moment with a particular group of students, that instructional decision is made in the context of the purpose of a lesson, the particular students a teacher is teaching, and the larger goals for learning. In talking with teachers and leaders alike, we saw how expanded goals for students that went beyond academic content and skills are in part what drove their commitment to project-based approaches. These goals became the central domains of our framework and help organize the chapters of this book. Next, we introduce each of the four goals in turn.

CORE GOALS AND CORE PRACTICES OF PROJECT-BASED TEACHING

Disciplinary: Cultivating Subject-Area Learning

While PBL can be a powerful engagement tool, we've heard again and again from accomplished PBL teachers that engagement isn't enough. If students are engaged but not learning something meaningful, PBL has failed in its mission. That's why the teachers that we've worked with have been so adamant with us that PBL is powerful only when it's leveraged in the explicit service of disciplinary or interdisciplinary learning goals. After all, it isn't teaching and learning if you're not teaching and learning *something*. But for a lot of teachers, the work of moving away from tests and lectures can feel like moving away from the content. These teachers have often asked us, "Doesn't something have to give? When we center students, don't we have to decenter content?" The answer to these questions is a definitive no, but keeping both content and students central in the classroom is complex work. It requires teachers to engage students in authentic, collaborative tasks that are full of choice and opportunities for personal connection, but atop this, *to continually pull students back to disciplinary habits of thinking*. The teachers we saw who did this well, tended to do three things:

- They elicited higher-order thinking.
  They didn't just split up students to work independently on projects; they circulated as students worked, asking questions that prompted students to evaluate, analyze, test, or critique, or they explicitly designed this kind of thinking into the tasks they gave students.

- They oriented students to subject-area content.
  In their design of tasks and in their interactions with students, teachers kept bringing core disciplinary understandings, key concepts, or big ideas back to the center of students' attention.

- They engaged students in disciplinary practices.

  Rather than treating projects as opportunities to learn facts, teachers consistently and explicitly engaged students in the habits of thinking that are core to the work of the professionals who work in the focal disciplinary domain. Accomplished PBL science teachers didn't get students to memorize scientific facts. Instead, they engaged students in thinking like scientists and in doing the kinds of things that scientists do.

Think back to Ms. Johnson's twelfth-grade government class, the class we visited at the start of this chapter. She had designed a project that she knew her students would find engaging: writing political action plans for local interest groups. While she knew the project would *engage* her students, without a skilled teacher focused on disciplinary learning at the helm, her students might not learn much about government. It's easy to imagine a world in which Ms. Johnson's students write political action plans that pay little or no attention to how their plan interacts with the elected institutions of government, the bureaucracy, and the budget—topics central to any government course. For students to get the most out of her project, Ms. Johnson has to consistently ask questions that (1) elicit higher-order thinking, (2) orient students to the content, and (3) engage students in the habits of thinking that policy-making requires. As she circulated around the classroom, to one group, she asked, "Which elected officials will need to pass judgment on the items you're proposing? Who are their constituents?" To another, she raised this question, "What are the budgetary implications of your proposal? Which budgets are implicated and who controls them?" To a third, she inquired, "Which city offices will need to be involved in these plans? Are the leaders of those offices elected or appointed? If appointed, who appointed them, and will they need to be reappointed? If elected, who elected them, and will they need to be reelected?" When Ms. Johnson asks questions like these—questions that keep content central, elicit higher-order thought, and force students into disciplinary habits of thinking—she transforms project-based learning from an *engagement* strategy ("I do PBL to keep my students active and engaged") into an engaging *learning* strategy ("I do PBL to engage students in meaningful content learning").

Authentic: Creating Relevant Experiences

As adults, we prove what we know and are able to do through engaging in *authentic* tasks—tasks with real purposes, real consequences, and real meaning; tasks, in other words, that make a real contribution to the world. Plumbers prove their skill when they fix leaking pipes. Doctors prove their knowledge when they diagnose and treat our ailments. Poets prove their craft when their writing evokes our emotions. In the adult world, we judge people's knowledge and skill by assessing the extent to which they're able to accomplish things that matter. Why, then, do we prepare young people for their adult lives by asking them, over and over again, to engage in tasks that have no real meaning, no real audience, and that contribute to the world in no meaningful way? What does a handout accomplish? Whom does a test benefit? To whom does an essay that only your teacher will ever read make a contribution? An education system that relies on inauthentic tasks to assess students' knowledge and skill has forgotten that the purpose of schooling is to prepare young people to do meaningful work in the world—work, in other words, that is *authentic.*

The accomplished PBL teachers that we have worked with are adamant about the need for students' work to extend beyond classroom walls and have real meaning for students and their communities. While all the educators' approaches to this goal are unique to their contexts and their worldviews, we've seen a few common practices that are shared across many of these teachers:

- They engage students in authentic disciplinary practices.
  Rather than asking students to learn *about* history or *about* science, they ask students to *do* history and to *do* science—to engage in the work of scientists and historians. They get into the archives and into the laboratory. They run their own experiments and examine historical artifacts. They play the game; they don't sit on the sidelines and watch it.

- They support students to build personal connections to their work.
  They ask students to share their personal opinions about the work in which they're engaged. They push students to consider topics in light of their own experiences, beliefs, or interests. They consistently come back to questions about what the work means to the students themselves.

- They support students to make a contribution to the world.
  They ensure that there are real audiences for the work that students do—
  and in many cases, not just audiences, but *consequences*. Rather than collect tests and essays that only they will read, accomplished PBL teachers
  design projects that will be shared with people in the community and
  may make a real contribution to addressing a real problem or need.

Remember Ms. Johnson—the teacher whose twelfth-grade government students were busy writing (or at least trying to start writing) political action plans for local interest groups? She had worked hard over several
years to get this project to the place where it was—and it was nowhere
near perfect. She had been an early adopter of the Knowledge in Action
Advanced Placement government curriculum several years before—a
project-based curriculum designed around a series of simulations.[6] Her
AP students had loved the simulations, and she'd seen their scores on the
AP test improve, but when she decided to adapt the curriculum for her
non-AP government courses, she wanted to make her students' work even
more authentic. She wanted to see whether she could replace the simulations with real-world activity by bringing the projects into her local community. The change didn't happen overnight—in fact, it took years—but
she slowly built partnerships with enough local interest groups to keep
all of her students busy. She partnered with a neighborhood alliance that
was interested in tackling problems associated with absentee landlords, a
public health organization that was interested in getting the city's health
department to certify HIV community health workers, and a local historical society that wanted to launch a campaign in partnership with city
government identifying important sites in local African American history. With these partnerships in place, she was no longer the audience
for her students' work; she was merely an editor and a coach, supporting
them to communicate their ideas to their real audience and to help them
design plans that might make a real contribution to their local community. Rather than learning *about* bureaucracy, budgets, and coalitions, her
students were meeting with city officials, crafting budgets, and building
coalitions. They were *doing* the work. And on top of that, it was work they

cared about, work in their local community, work that affected them and their families on a tangible level.

Collaborative: Building Student Agency in Learning Communities

Work that makes an impact is rarely accomplished by a lone wolf. Houses, bridges, and roads are built by crews. Patients are treated by teams. Communities are governed by associations. In an increasingly complex world, it is rare to find individuals accomplishing great feats entirely independently. Even when we work alone, it is usually so that we can pass off what we have accomplished to others so that they can add to it or use it in some way. Why, then, in so many classrooms, is the goal independence rather than interdependence? If being able to "do it independently" is the goal we have for our students, we have set our bar too low. The procedures that surgeons can perform independently are less sophisticated than the ones they can perform with teams. The bridges that engineers can design and build by themselves will get us across creeks and not raging rivers. Embracing collaborative work allows us to embrace bigger goals and grander dreams. One student can't plan and implement a youth arts festival that takes over the town commons, but an entire class of students can. One student can't partner with the local historical society, engage local government, and fundraise enough money to install a series of "youth that made history" plaques around town, but an advisory group of students can. Think of the incredible things that could get accomplished in your community with a team of thirty people who each had ten hours a week to dedicate to the work. If you're a teacher, you already have that team. What will you lead them to accomplish?

Accomplished PBL teachers see classrooms as interdependent spaces where students work together in pursuit of goals that they simply couldn't accomplish all on their own. In these classrooms, students divvy up big tasks and take on specialized roles; they negotiate ideas, plans, and wording; they ask each other for the help (and sometimes for the space) they need to accomplish tasks. In other words, they collaborate. Creating a classroom where this kind of work takes place, however, is challenging. It requires teachers to engage in practices that spark a culture of collaboration and that then keep that culture alive through all of the trials that inevitably accompany interdependence. While each teacher is different, the practices that we've seen from accomplished PBL teachers are these:

- They support students to make choices.

   They know that students are motivated to engage in tasks that they feel ownership over, not tasks where they are filling in the blanks of someone else's choices. In the many moments when choices need to be made in the classroom, they resist making the choices themselves and offer students explicit supports for making big (and small) decisions about the processes and the products of their work.

- They support students to collaborate.

   They support students as they define their roles and responsibilities, design and manage thoughtful group processes, and reflect on and refine their collaborative efforts. They offer scaffolds and structure for collaboration. They closely monitor participation and communication, and they intervene when necessary. In addition, they offer models, prompts, and other resources to ensure students are building their capacity to work effectively together.

In Ms. Johnson's class, groups were collaborating with varying levels of success. This was true every year she attempted this project. There was always one group that worked together effortlessly, a few that hit a few rough patches and persisted, and one or two that struggled mightily. Over the years, she had learned to anticipate these struggles. During classes where students spent most of the period engaged in group work, the period always began with Ms. Johnson asking students to set teamwork goals. Some students committed to asking for help from classmates, some committed to making someone else on their team look good, some committed to raising concerns early. Students selected these goals from a list of "aspects of effective teamwork" that lived on an anchor chart in the front of the room and that had been growing since the beginning of the year. It started with findings from research on team effectiveness and grew as students identified more aspects of effective teamwork each time they ran postmortems on group projects. Next, Ms. Johnson led the class in a three-minute check-in routine where group members decided on their unique responsibilities for the day and identified areas where they would need to work together to accomplish something during that period. Groupwork classes always ended with an exit slip where students reflected on how well their team had functioned and three minutes of teamwork shout-outs during which students commended each other for concrete things they had done to further the goals of the team and to make the team look good. Even when engaged in these routines, some groups still struggled, and Ms. Johnson had to engage in collaboration triage frequently as she circulated, but she saw this as a part of the process rather than as a failure of her own, her students, or groupwork in general.

Iterative: Cultivating a Culture of Production, Feedback, Reflection, and Revision

Think of something you have accomplished that you learned a lot doing and that you are proud of. You taught yourself a complex piece on the piano that you never thought you'd be able to play the whole way through without stopping. You trained for months and beat your 5K personal record. After several rejections, you got a poem published in a literary journal. You crafted and recrafted a curricular unit until it got your students excited about the content. You finally knit a sweater that you could wear without being embarrassed. Whatever came to mind for you—whatever it was that you learned from and that made you proud—chances are it didn't take you fifty minutes to complete. You probably didn't get it perfect on your first try. In fact, you probably had to try it a lot of times before you were done. You probably tested a lot of different approaches before you hit on the one that worked. And, chances are, at some point you got some help from someone else. Why? Because that's how learning works. Which is why it's astonishing that in so many classrooms whatever students get done by the end of the period is turned in to the teacher and never seen again, except when it's returned with a final grade on it.

For the teachers we've worked with who are the most accomplished in their PBL practice, first drafts are never final drafts. Each day in the classroom is an opportunity to come back to a problem or a task that's too complex to tackle in one sitting. For these teachers, classrooms are places for prototyping and drafting, for revising and revisiting, and sometimes, even, for beginning again. This kind of teaching, however, is complex. It requires teachers to engage in practices that keep a culture of iteration alive. The practices that we've seen again and again among the most accomplished PBL teachers are these:

- They track student progress and provide feedback.

  Rather than collecting and grading students' completed classwork and homework each day, they keep track of students' ongoing work—work that extends across days, weeks, or even months. In this model, feedback isn't simply a rationale for a grade; instead, it's useful, suggesting where students can take the work next and how they can improve what they already have.

- They support students to give and receive feedback.

  They know that students can learn as much from examining others' work as they do from focusing on their own. They create lots of opportunities for students to see and critique each other's in-progress work. They also understand that giving and receiving feedback are skills that people need support to learn, and they offer students strong supports for both activities.

- They support students to reflect and revise.

  They know that bulldozing your way through a project without stopping to consider how it's going, to adjust your plans, and to make changes is never the way to the best final product. Because of this, they carve out lots of time and create lots of supports for students to reflect on their pathway and their progress and to revise their plans and their work.

In Ms. Johnson's classroom, identifying when students *weren't* iterating was easier than identifying when they *were*. The reason is that the spirit of iteration was so deeply infused in everything that she did that it seems as though it was always present. Rather than consistently turning their work in to the teacher for evaluation, students prepared instead for a series of workshops where they shared with others the work they had done thus far and engaged in cycles of feedback, reflection, and revision. Students needed to come to the budgeting workshop with a draft of their budget, for example, and they needed to come to the coalition-building workshop with a draft of their coalition-building plan. And while some of these workshops were entirely student-run, at others, outside experts came in to give feedback to one group at a time as the rest of the class watched and took notes. In addition to the workshops, Ms. Johnson's students ended most class periods by writing short reflections on where they were in relationship to their goals, both big and small, and she used these reflections whenever she checked in with groups. Because of these routines, Ms. Johnson's students rarely stayed up all night working before big deadlines. The reason wasn't that her students were unusually diligent, though. It was that she had structured cycles of iteration into her instruction so seamlessly that, without even knowing it sometimes, students often began work on big projects months before they were due. By the time these projects were complete, there had always been many different eyes on the work, many first drafts thrown in the trash bin, and many improvements made along the way.

GOING DEEPER

While Ms. Johnson's classroom is a shining example of the core practices in action, no classroom context is the same. A million different things influence what can and what should happen for a particular group of students. From our research, however, we've found one factor that remains constant across teachers who do this kind of work well: the mindsets that teachers bring with them into the classroom. Practices never exist in a vacuum but are always shaped both by the beliefs that teachers bring to their work and the contexts in which they work. In our work with teachers, we began to see that successful teachers of PBL shared a set of beliefs about students, about the purposes of education, and about their own work as teachers that helped them enact project-based learning. Project-based learning takes considerable time and energy. To invest this time, teachers generally believe that the goal of school is to cultivate a wide range of learning, including developing a deep understanding of content rather than a focus on more surface-level knowledge, the ability to work with others toward common goals, and nurturing student agency rather than students taking a passive role to their own education. As one teacher told us, "This broader array of goals supports the investment of time that PBL requires." Teachers also share a belief that students are capable of directing their learning and of making significant contributions to their community. As another teacher told us, "The whole idea of project-based learning is to get the students to see that the work they do is important not just for learning but for the betterment of themselves, their community, and the society they live in." Yet another teacher provided a rich explanation of motivations to invest in PBL:

> I think part of it was because, or mostly because, I felt like it really is what engages students in real work and meaningful work. I just felt like the worksheets and the tests just made school feel like a factory. That even if kids were learning things in order to complete a worksheet or do well on a test, it was something that they were going to forget the next day, or the next week, or the next year. What was really going to stay with the kids were some of the more ... social-emotional skills that are easier to incorporate into the projects. Things like follow-through, and persistence and pursuing something through frustration. Getting a really deep understanding of something. Getting a whole variety of perspectives on something. Having to work with other people ... and I felt like projects, really, were the only way to do it.

Teachers also need to trust in students' capability to support each other's learning, that the teacher is not the only source of knowledge or support in the room. This belief drives teachers' efforts to build strong norms around student collaboration and interdependence. As one PBL teacher told us:

> Perhaps one of the biggest transitions for teachers into a PBL environment is to relinquish a sense of authority in order to support

student voice in the classroom. From the first day of school in the ninth grade I am working to build student choice, voice, and agency in all classroom activities.

We heard from teachers that this shift to decentering the teacher as the primary source of authority and direction was one of the most challenging shifts they faced in moving toward more project-based classrooms. To persevere, they had to believe and trust in student capacity, in addition to having the strategies and skills to support students as they develop the necessary agency and collaborative skills to take on new levels of responsibility.

The teachers with whom we talked also held a deep equity stance toward their work, believing that all students deserved opportunities to have agency over their learning. As noted previously, one of the persistent inequities in our education system is the differential access to such ambitious kinds of learning and the belief by some that students in high poverty-impacted communities cannot succeed in such settings. In fact, we have seen multiple instances in which teachers in poverty-impacted urban contexts are providing students with exactly these kinds of opportunities. Oftentimes, this work is driven by concerns for equity and an imperative to enact PBL in urban schools that serve predominantly students of color. The Workshop School and the Science Leadership Academy network of schools are public schools within the School District of Philadelphia offering rich opportunities for PBL to students living in poverty. The Washington Heights Expeditionary Learning School (WHEELS) in New York serves as another example of a school committed to creating expanded and experiential learning opportunities for PreK–12 students in the context of a poverty-impacted urban district. Our hope is to make such examples more commonplace than rare in districts across the country.

Finally, accomplished project-based teachers also recognize that their students are not the only ones on a learning journey; they are as well. They saw their own work as teachers as an on-going project that required constant iteration and reflection, as well as collaboration with their peers. Teachers spoke about learning from student feedback as well as the importance of finding communities of practice that supported their work. Many of the PBL schools we visited take teacher learning as seriously as they take student learning, building multiple opportunities for teachers to work and learn together. School leaders saw their role as supporting teachers' opportunities to learn and grow in the practice of project-based learning. Given the complexity of project-based teaching, a learning stance may be particularly important, as teachers new to this type of teaching begin to implement new curricula, new instructional activities, and new norms and routines.

Ultimately, we hope that this framework provides an opportunity for teachers and leaders who are interested in enacting PBL to come together to learn about and improve their instruction. In the chapters that follow, we will take you deeper into the practices we previewed in this chapter and, along the way, we will offer windows into a number of different classrooms. Each teacher we spotlight takes a different approach to the core practices of PBL. Each approach is unique to them and to the needs of their students and their community. Chapters 2 through 5 each focus on one of our four core goals and discuss the core practices associated with each goal in greater detail. In chapter 6, we discuss how the teachers that we have worked with pull all of the practices together in their work with students. In chapter 7, we explore the many ways that we've seen teachers work together to improve their PBL practice. Here (and also in the appendix) we offer a few spotlights on particular schools and organizations that have developed innovative ways to support teachers and schools as they grow their capacity in this work.

Our hope is that readers will receive our description of these practices in the spirit they are offered, not as prescriptions or instructions, but as visions of the possible. From these visions of practice, we invite you to take the things that will unlock possibilities in your own context, to look past those things that will not work for you, and to use what we share as a springboard to imagine versions of practice that move the ideas we share in this book even further than we have yet been able to imagine.

— TWO —

Keeping the Discipline in View

*Practices That Cultivate
Subject-Area Learning*

"Five minutes is simply not enough time," Jenelle says emphatically. All the students nod their heads in agreement, except Crystal, who clearly looks unconvinced. "Do you disagree, Crystal?" probes Ms. Lopez. "I do!" Crystal fires back. "I'm never late for class! Five minutes is more than enough!" Ms. Lopez can't help but smile, knowing her middle school math class is about to dive into a heated debate, which is exactly what she was hoping for.

"I have to walk all the way from the north wing to the south wing between third and fourth period. That's a passing period for lunch. . . . Have you ever tried getting past everyone rushing into the cafeteria? I'm telling you; it's impossible," offers another student. Several others express their agreement. "So, what *would* be possible?" Ms. Lopez asks. "What do you mean?" several students counter at once. "I mean, if five minutes isn't possible, then what would be?"

After a brief pause, Sean offers, "It's impossible to know. Everyone is different." Unsatisfied with the response, Ms. Lopez follows up, "Say more, Sean."

After a moment to gather his thoughts, and fully aware that all eyes are on him, he offers, "Well, nearly every student has a different situation. They are traveling to different classrooms. Everyone needs a different amount of time."

With a tinge of frustration, Crystal pushes back, "So what does that mean? It's different for everyone, so we just don't have passing periods? How would that work?" Several students start talking immediately. Ms. Lopez uses this as an opportunity to pivot the classroom energy into a quick check-in within student groups. "Okay, one sec. Hold up! The question on the table is if five minutes isn't possible, what would be? Given that each student has a different circumstance, what would work? Take three minutes to discuss what you think with your group."

After three minutes, Ms. Lopez brings the class back and asks representatives from each group to share some highlights from their discussion. It's clear that most people in the class agree that a five-minute passing period isn't enough time, but it's also apparent that there is no consensus on what a "fair" solution would be. Ms. Lopez is clearly pleased by the lack of agreement, although it also seems that many students are a bit frustrated, having just realized that they are facing a problem that they hadn't before realized they were facing.

"For many of you, a five-minute passing period appears to feel a bit arbitrary at best, even unfair at worst. Where, exactly, did the five-minute rule come from?" The entire class is staring at Ms. Lopez as if she's about to reveal some dark deep secret. "In reality, the world is full of five-minute rules. How long should a stoplight be red? How fast should a speed limit be set? How long should a commercial break during your favorite TV show be? Many of these decisions are not arbitrary or random. Many of these are intentional decisions made by real people."

"But how?" Crystal asks. Pleased that someone finally set her up, Ms. Lopez exclaims, "By using mathematics!" Crystal sighs, "Ahh! I knew you were going to bring this back to math!" Ms. Lopez chuckles and then continues, "Yes—of course! Mathematics offers us a set of tools and problem-solving strategies to help us analyze problems and make thoughtful decisions. Therefore, we can use mathematics to explore this question of how long our passing periods should be."

Ms. Lopez hands out the project description and expectations sheet as she begins to highlight some of the details. "One week from today, Principal Foster will join us in class." Ms. Lopez pauses, for dramatic effect, as several students perk up. "She is curious to hear *your* recommendation for what we should do about the passing periods for next school year." Crystal chimes in, "Wait . . . seriously?" Ms. Lopez continues, "Absolutely! But keep in mind, Principal Foster isn't going to be convinced without strong, solid, mathematical arguments. Your job, as a team, will be to determine a recommendation and justify it using mathematics."

As Ms. Lopez finishes describing the task, students turn inward to start discussing the project within their teams. As outlined in the project expectations, each group has to gather six data points—walking times between six pairs of locations—to use in their final argument. Along with the data, the project card prompts students to consider Ethos, Pathos, and Logos as they plan their presentation for Principal Foster.

Over the next few days, students eagerly prepare their presentations. The chance to propose a real policy change to Principal Foster is a task that nearly everyone takes seriously. The fact that she will be in the room listening to their arguments (a fact that Ms. Lopez constantly reminds everyone about) provides a clear sense of meaning and purpose behind their work. Students even talk up the project to their friends and their family. As a class, they gather a total of thirty-six data points that describe the time required to walk between six pairs of locations. Some groups decide to average the data points for a given pair of locations, and others create graphs and charts to show the range of times. While many of the data points fall well below the five-minute mark, a handful do in fact exceed it. Students work tirelessly on creating beautiful PowerPoint presentations and practicing their speeches as they prepare for Principal Foster's visit.

Taking a Step Back

Throughout this project, Ms. Lopez acknowledges that she experienced some of the highest levels of student engagement all year. Students were genuinely interested, actively participated, and even talked about the project outside of class. But as she takes a step back to reflect, she wonders: did math students actually learn? Sure, her students made measurements and collected data. But on their own, Ms. Lopez knows that those activities do not elicit higher-order thinking. In fact, many of these skills might best fit under lower elementary math standards, not middle school math standards, which is the focus of this course. Some groups calculated averages and created graphs, but again, those skills are far below grade-level standards. While students do engage in argumentation, the focus here is on rhetoric and persuasion, not using data and evidence to justify a mathematical claim.

So, what exactly is going on here? Ms. Lopez knows that several parts of this project seemed to be working well. It had a compelling question, an investigation, an authentic audience, a "public" presentation, and a clear personal connection to the work. However, this project failed to engage students in rich disciplinary work, the type of work Ms. Lopez knows is so important for her students as they develop an empowering and broad appreciation for mathematics. She wonders how she could revise this project so that it incorporates opportunities for ambitious mathematical learning.

Revising for Disciplinary Thinking

A year has gone by and Ms. Lopez looks forward to the next iteration of the passing period project. As she considers the ambitious mathematical goals she has for her students, she considers what changes she can make to the project. If she wants her students to think, question, explore, and argue like mathematicians, how can she modify the project to make that possible? Instead of outlining a prescriptive process to students (e.g., to gather a predetermined set of data points), Ms. Lopez decides to frame the task in a more open-ended way. She will have students develop a mathematical model that predicts travel time, use the model to analyze several scenarios, and use their analysis to develop a mathematical argument for Principal Foster. This work directly engages students in several mathematical practices as well as helps them begin to appreciate the power that mathematical tools can bring to a problem-solving process.

Ms. Lopez decides that the first task will be for students to generate a list of likely variables that would go into their mathematical models. Because these variables are not predescribed, each group may identify a different set of considerations. For example, one group might include the time of day and walking distance in their model, while another group may include walking speed and the number of "social interactions" (e.g., stop-and-chats) students have on their journey. Through a process of peer review and feedback, groups may decide to modify and change the variables they include in their model, as they learn from their peers.

Next, Ms. Lopez will have students gather real data that helps them determine the relationships between the variables, and eventually develop a set of functions that help predict walking time between any two points in the school. After several rounds of testing, they can begin to determine how useful—and elegant—their models are at accurately predicting walking time. They might determine that some variables play a more significant role in their model (e.g., total walking distance), whereas others turn out to be less significant (e.g., year of the student). Through this process of testing, they will continue to refine their models.

Now equipped with mathematical models, Ms. Lopez will have students explore a variety of cases to generate data on walking time. Because they have a mathematical model, students will be able to produce many more data points for many more cases than they would be able to gather by direct measurement. They will also be able to produce more nuanced insights, such as the distance between room N305 and W201 ranges between three minutes and six minutes, depending on walking speed, time of day, and whether or not the student stops at the water fountain.

Finally, students will be ready to make confident claims, backed by sophisticated mathematical reasoning, in their presentations to Principal Foster. Ms. Lopez is quite curious to know whether Principal Foster will see a difference in the sophistication of the mathematical arguments she hears, compared to last year.

While these two versions of the project share many of the same features, Ms. Lopez appreciates how her updated version clearly creates many more opportunities for students to engage with significant mathematical ideas, and actually engage in mathematical practices, throughout their inquiry.

Ms. Lopez's example illustrates an idea that is central to this book. Some educators critique project-based learning because it fails to offer disciplinary rigor. However, engaging students in rich disciplinary learning is a central goal of project-based learning. Like Ms. Lopez, we as educators must be deliberate and intentional in creating rich opportunities to engage in disciplinary learning within our projects. We see this type of disciplinary engagement as central to our definition of project-based learning.

DISCIPLINARY GOALS AND PRACTICES

Defining the Disciplinary Goal and Practices

One of the persistent critiques of project-based learning has been its lack of attention to disciplinary knowledge and practices. All too often, projects might engage students with enjoyable activities and result in high levels of student engagement but fail to help students grapple with meaningful content or exercise skills that are characteristics of the disciplines. As in the preceding example, students can successfully complete a project, collaborate around an authentic task, and present to an authentic audience all without developing the requisite mathematical knowledge and practices for a particular grade level or content area. However, as one PBL expert with whom we spoke adamantly argued:

> Project-based learning is only effective if it addresses key learning standards and subject matter central to the discipline; projects created for "projects-sake" only are misguided and "fluff." However, high levels of content knowledge and pedagogical content knowledge are required for pedagogues to craft learning experiences that address key content and skill learning through an educational experience that is rigorous and results in authentic products. This type of teaching also requires great flexibility and responsiveness to students' needs.

Our own definition of project-based learning emphasizes the importance of providing rich opportunities for content and disciplinary learning and making such learning accessible to all students. We also agree that PBL places demands on teachers' own content knowledge and ability to translate that knowledge into rich learning activities and assessments. In the preceding scenario, the second version of the project requires Ms. Lopez to have a much stronger grasp of the mathematics herself. As students engage in the process of developing and refining mathematical models, using those models to make predictions, and constructing mathematical arguments, they will undoubtedly benefit from a great deal of coaching, feedback, and prompting. The ability to be responsive and supportive as students generate unique ideas will be in part dependent on Ms. Lopez's familiarity with mathematics, the common misconceptions students have, and ways to help students develop deeper understandings of complex ideas. In this chapter, we unpack some of the practices that support this vision of PBL grounded in disciplinary content as well as the demands on teachers' subject matter knowledge.

Designing Opportunities to Engage in Disciplinary Knowledge and Practices

Ensuring the disciplinary integrity of PBL begins, not surprisingly, with project design. As noted in the example at the beginning of this chapter, projects can be designed to either feature or sideline rich opportunities to delve into content learning, so creating projects with disciplinary learning in mind from the outset is critical. There are many resources for teachers to find high-quality projects within their content areas; see appendix A for some ideas for getting started.

One example of a project-based curriculum designed around rich disciplinary learning opportunities is the Knowledge in Action curricula designed as an alternative to the Advanced Placement courses in Environmental Science and Government and Politics. The courses are designed around an overarching question that motivates the integration of content. In the KIA version of the AP US Government and Politics course, the question is "What is the proper role of government in a democracy?" In the Environmental Science course, the driving question is "How can we live more sustainably?" These courses contain the same content covered in more traditional AP classes but develop students' knowledge and skills through engagement in a set of carefully designed projects. Of course, in addition to the disciplinary content, these classes also aim to develop the other goals of PBL, including collaboration, student agency, and in these cases, students' understanding of their role as citizens.

Social studies projects at the elementary level can support students to research their own families' histories and to put their families' stories into larger historical narratives. Often these projects can include interviewing family members to access oral histories and contextualizing these personal stories into the broader historical trends connected to waves of immigration, migration, forced enslavement, and settler colonialism. Understanding their families' stories and how they connect to broader historical narratives, students can create collections of stories or art pieces that depict both personal and national trends. Such a project provides rich opportunities to develop an understanding of one aspect of American history, while also developing the ability to access and read historical documents and collect oral histories, practices that are characteristic of the work historians do. Such a project is also filled with opportunities to talk about counter-narratives to the dominant American story, cultural differences in how we define families, and how racism underlies so much of this history.

But as we argued in our introduction, access to high-quality curriculum and projects is not sufficient to guarantee that students will actually engage deeply with the opportunities to learn content. As we've learned from years of research and practice, the enacted curriculum—the curriculum students actually receive—can differ substantially from what was initially designed, depending on how teachers use the resources. To ensure students actually develop the disciplinary knowledge and practices, teachers also need to employ a set of instructional practices that support this goal. These practices include (1) eliciting higher-order thinking, (2) orienting students to subject area content, and (3) engaging students in disciplinary practices. (See figure 2.1.)

FIGURE 2.1 Disciplinary practices

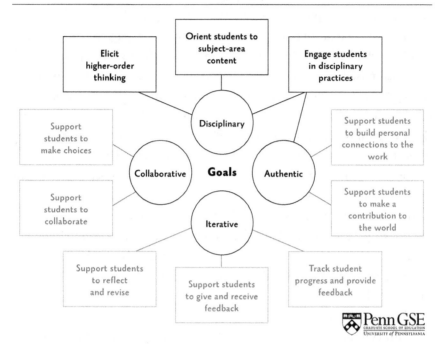

Source: Pam Grossman, Christopher Pupik Dean, Sarah Schneider Kavanagh, and Zachary Herrmann. "Preparing Teachers for Project-Based Teaching." kappanonline.org, March 25, 2019. https://kappanonline.org/preparing-teachers-project-based-teaching-grossman-pupik-dean-kavanagh-herrmann/.

CORE PRACTICE
ELICIT HIGHER-ORDER THINKING

As illustrated by the scenario that opens this chapter, a critical role of teachers in PBL is to push students to move beyond rote learning and to press for students to engage in higher-order thinking. Rather than have students solve preset equations, Ms. Lopez pressed them to generate a range of variables that might account for the optimal length of a passing period and to develop mathematical models to propose solutions. She asked students to develop arguments for their proposals complete with mathematical justifications. The project itself pressed students to think critically about the problem of an ideal passing period.

To some extent, opportunities for students to engage in higher-order thinking can be baked into curriculum design through the projects and activities posed for students. For example, in one of the first units of the KIA AP Government and Policy curriculum, students are asked to participate in a simulation of the Constitutional Convention of 1787. By taking on different roles, they begin to understand the perspective of delegates and their stances toward the Constitution. They learn to read historical documents, including the Declaration of Independence and other primary sources, to understand the issues confronting the framers of the Constitution and some of the tensions around federalism and the relationship between the federal government and states' rights. Beyond learning facts about the formation of American democracy, they are learning to develop historical understanding, read primary source documents, and take on different perspectives, all examples of higher-order thinking in history.

However, accomplished PBL teachers do not rely solely on the project itself to prompt higher-order thinking. Rather, these teachers continually engage with their students throughout the course of a project, prompting and challenging them to think deeply about the content. Even when projects are designed to invite students into thinking critically about the subject matter, teachers and students alike can find themselves focusing more on superficial features of the content or swerving away from content altogether as they engage in project tasks. One of the reasons for orienting a project around an essential question is to remind students to continue to ask themselves how the research they're doing relates to the broader question. One strategy PBL teachers can use is explicitly prompting students to make these connections back to the essential question. Encouraging students to consider these questions supports their ability to synthesize information, make claims, and generate evidence to support those claims.

Much of the work teachers do to press for higher-order thinking within a discipline happens in whole group discussion, in which teachers can ask students to defend their claims or synthesize different perspectives as part of the larger discussion. Teachers can use a variety of what have been referred to as "talk moves" to support students' efforts to engage in higher-order thinking. For example, in their work in mathematics classrooms, Suzanne Chapin, Catherine O'Connor, and Nancy Anderson describe how teachers can use moves like asking students to paraphrase each other's contributions to a discussion or to agree or disagree with peers and providing reasons as ways to prompt students to engage in productive thought and discussion.[1] In work on ambitious science teaching, Mark Windschitl, Jessica Thompson, and Melissa Braaten have developed a set of practices and tools to help students engage in higher-order thinking around science in classroom discussions, including *pressing for evidence-based explanations* of scientific phenomena.[2]

Teachers also engage in this practice as they work with project teams. In monitoring students' progress, teachers often confer with groups to check in and provide support. These check-ins provide the opportunity for teachers to press groups for justifications around key decisions, to ask analytic questions, or to suggest fruitful new lines of inquiry. While teachers who don't teach with projects also press for critical thinking, project-based teachers can leverage aspects of the project, like the production of a public product, as tools to make this thinking more visible. For example, a popular project in secondary English classrooms involves producing a scene from a play. Prior to production, small groups are asked to engage in critical interpretive work around how lines might be read to convey particular emotions and relationships, how the play might be blocked to convey a particular interpretation, even in what time period the play might be set to highlight historical resonances to thematic elements. The production of the scene provides an opportunity to make this critical interpretive work public and for the audience to ask students to justify their choices through an interpretive lens.

The work teachers do to press students toward higher-order thinking makes good on the promise of project-based learning to challenge students intellectually *through* their work on projects. Research from the Trends in International Mathematics and Science Study (TIMSS) of videos of mathematics teaching in sixteen different countries found that there were distinctive differences in how teachers in different countries managed the intellectual challenge of mathematical tasks.[3] Teachers in some countries managed to maintain the challenge of the task while supporting students in attempting different strategies to solve the problem. Others, however, progressively made the task easier when students struggled, by reducing the complexity of the task or by providing answers to students, rather than strategies. Unfortunately, in American classrooms, teachers were often more likely to reduce the difficulty of the task over the course of a lesson. Part of the challenge in supporting students through a project-based curriculum is to ensure that the intellectual challenge and focus on disciplinary learning remain high. (See "Getting Started with Eliciting Higher-Order Thinking: Questions to Ask Yourself.")

CORE PRACTICE
ORIENT STUDENTS TO THE SUBJECT MATTER

Part of maintaining a focus on the disciplinary goals of a project requires teachers to continually orient students back to the subject matter goals of a project. If teachers fail to do this, students might develop creative and interesting projects that don't necessarily support them in developing rich content understandings. To return to our original example, Ms. Lopez's students might have turned their attention to generating passionate arguments about their own preferences for length of passing period and how to develop compelling PowerPoints to sway the principal's mind without ever really engaging in the mathematical content. Similarly, students could produce a scene from a play by reading their assigned roles without engaging in the interpretive work that is central to literary understanding. To maintain a focus on content, teachers need to begin a project by framing the subject matter goals, prompt students throughout the project to return to those goals, and assess projects according to how successfully students met the learning goals around content.

Getting Started with Eliciting Higher-Order Thinking:
QUESTIONS TO ASK YOURSELF

In thinking about an upcoming project or unit, consider the following questions:

Project design:

- How does the guiding question of a course or unit allow for moving beyond simple yes/no answers?

- To what extent does the project ask students to look for multiple perspectives, revise hypotheses, synthesize information, or evaluate evidence?

- How are different project tasks or activities linked back to the broader guiding question?

During discussion and work with small groups and teams:

- Are questions open-ended enough to allow for multiple responses and not just yes/no answers?

- To what extent are students raising questions and responding to each other's comments?

- Are teachers and students pressing for elaboration of response and counterarguments?

So how can teachers ensure that students don't lose track of the content as they engage in project-based learning? First, teachers can ensure the projects they choose are aligned with important content goals and that students are made aware of these goals from the beginning of a project. Part of the planning process can involve assessing the curricular potential of projects for helping students grapple with important ideas within a subject area. The passing period project, for example, provided students opportunities to learn about the predictive value of mathematical models, use such models to analyze possible solutions, and use data to provide mathematical justifications. By making these goals visible from the outset of a project, teachers can more easily reorient students to them as they move through their work.

In structuring tasks and assignments that make up the larger project and checking in with project teams, teachers can also remind students of the broader content goals related to more discrete project tasks. In the example of a project around family histories mentioned earlier, for example, students can get so excited about interviewing family members that they lose sight of connecting these personal stories to the larger history of migration in the United States. By structuring the need to link the individual stories with the larger national history into part of the task, teachers help students make this connection to the broader content goals. Teachers can do this through whole-class instruction and in consultations with project groups, redirecting them back to the content when necessary. Teachers can also provide a guide for peer review that specifically redirects peers to provide feedback on the content goals.

Teachers also need to make sure that their assessments make the disciplinary content visible and hold students accountable for meeting those goals. Project rubrics can articulate the expectations around both the content and disciplinary practices that students are expected to gain as a result of their work on projects and provide ongoing feedback about how well students are meeting those goals. Teachers can create interim checkpoints that allow teachers to track not only students' progress toward completing projects but also their progress toward understanding the content and mastering the tools of inquiry. Both these interim and final assessments keep the disciplinary goals visible to students and teachers alike. (See "Getting Started with Orienting Students to the Discipline: Questions to Ask Yourself.")

CORE PRACTICE
ENGAGE STUDENTS IN DISCIPLINARY PRACTICES

In traditional classrooms, students have plenty of opportunities to see the insights and knowledge produced by scientists, historians, mathematicians,

> ### Getting Started with Orienting Students to the Discipline:
> ## QUESTIONS TO ASK YOURSELF
>
> In thinking about an upcoming project or unit, consider the following questions:
>
> Content focus:
>
> - How is the project tied to subject matter goals for my students? What are the most important knowledge, skills, and practices within one or more disciplines that I want students to develop through this project?
> - How is the need to develop these skills and knowledge built into the project tasks and activities?
>
> Highlighting content throughout the project:
>
> - How can I use mini-lessons or group meetings to highlight the disciplinary content of a project? At what point in the trajectory of a project would it be helpful to highlight disciplinary goals?
>
> Assessment:
>
> - How will I assess whether students achieved the subject matter goals through their work on projects?

and writers. However, much of the student experience is akin to sitting on the sidelines, watching others play. The reason is that students tend to have more opportunities to learn about the knowledge produced by others rather than producing the knowledge themselves. They are watching the game; they aren't playing it. If we expect our students to develop into critical and capable leaders, ready for the challenges facing both themselves and their communities, they need opportunities to be knowledge producers in their own right. Rather than merely learning about science, they need opportunities to *do* science. Rather than learning about math, they need opportunities to *think and act* like mathematicians. Rather than learning about technology, they need opportunities to *problem-solve* like engineers. In other words, rather than simply learning the knowledge of the disciplines, students need opportunities to consider the problems that disciplinarians are working on and engage in the actual practices of the disciplines. (See "On the Sidelines or Playing the Game?")

Enabling students to learn in this way involves creating opportunities for them to engage in questions that are specific to a discipline by using the methods of that discipline. For example, the elementary project involving immigration poses a problem of historical significance to students and then supports students in using the tools of historical inquiry to approach that problem. In a similar project that deals with immigration, for example, a teacher might ask her eighth-grade students to prepare and lead a simulation about Ellis Island for fifth graders at their school, providing an opportunity to learn about one aspect of immigration and then represent what they've learned to an authentic audience. The teacher might begin by asking an authentic question that a historian might ask: What was the experience like for immigrants as they navigated their way through Ellis Island? To answer this question, students engage in doing what a historian would do to answer it, reading through primary sources and assessing the reliability of each account by examining the source of the document, contextualizing it, and corroborating it with other primary sources. In this way, students are engaging in historical inquiry, using the tools and practices of the discipline, as they learn about the experiences of immigrants at Ellis Island.

ON THE SIDELINES OR PLAYING THE GAME?

Examples of students on the sidelines	Examples of students playing the game
• Students follow the directions of a "science lab" to replicate the results that have already been verified by others.	• Students observe a puzzling phenomenon, develop a hypothesis, and design and run an experiment to test their hypothesis.
• Students read examples of news articles and analyze the structure and writing techniques used in those articles.	• Students write an article about an issue in their school and submit it to the school newspaper.
• Students create a timeline of events around the American Revolution based on information in their textbook.	• Students read and analyze primary source documents that present conflicting timelines of events around the American Revolution and must determine which is more likely to be accurate.

In the mathematical example that opened this chapter, Ms. Lopez creates a project that requires students to think like mathematicians: to identify variables, develop models that describe the relationship among variables, and then test the models using empirical data, all examples of mathematical practices. In many ways, engaging students in these disciplinary practices can be the most powerful part of working on projects, as they provide the intellectual tools that will fuel future learning and allow students to generate knowledge.

Highlighting the kinds of practices students are developing and naming them can be an important part of students developing an intellectual toolkit for the future. For example, knowing why historians always begin with identifying the source of a primary source document and understanding what perspective might accompany the source, as well as developing practice in identifying and questioning sources, will help students be better equipped for looking at primary source documents in the future. (See "Getting Started with Engaging Students in Disciplinary Practices: Questions to Ask Yourself.")

Disciplinary inquiry is important to project-based teachers even when projects are *inter*disciplinary, as so many projects are. In the next section, we explore what these disciplinary goals and practices mean in the context of interdisciplinary work.

Disciplinary Goals for Interdisciplinary Curricula

Although much of this chapter has focused on projects that prioritize learning within a single discipline, we recognize that many people first think about interdisciplinary projects when they think about PBL, in part because projects can naturally lend themselves to learning across multiple subject matter domains. Particularly in elementary school, teachers often create projects that cross subject matter boundaries, providing opportunities for students to delve into scientific explorations even as they develop their reading and writing skills. For example, the Multiple Literacies in Project-Based Learning program, developed by Joseph Krajcik, Annemarie Palincsar, and Emily Miller, provides opportunities for students to develop scientific understanding while also developing literacy and numeracy

Getting Started with Engaging Students in Disciplinary Practices:
QUESTIONS TO ASK YOURSELF

In thinking about an upcoming project or unit, consider the following questions:

Disciplinary inquiry:

- What is the fundamental disciplinary question or problem that this unit explores?

- What resources, tools, processes, or technologies do people in this discipline or field use to tackle this question or problem? (Examples might include the use of the scientific method, of mathematical models, of authentication of sources.)

- Where are the opportunities to remind students of how their work on this project is linked to larger disciplinary problems?

Disciplinary talk:

- How might scholars within a discipline talk about the content being explored?

- What vocabulary and concepts must students have access to in order to engage in disciplinary talk?

- Where in the project trajectory are opportunities for students to use the vocabulary and concepts that disciplinarians use to talk with one another and to me about their work? How can I support and encourage this kind of talk?

skills; each project is designed from the outset with these different content areas in mind.[4] An elementary school project that asks students to write a piece of historical fiction based on some aspect of American history is another example of an interdisciplinary project that provides opportunities to develop understandings related to both history and literature, as well as practices of historical inquiry and narrative writing.

All these sample projects draw on multiple disciplines, in contrast to the earlier descriptions of projects that centered on a single content area of mathematics, literature, or history. Let's look more closely at the project that asked students to create a work of historical fiction. (See "Creating a Work of Historical Fiction.") Such a project has the potential to help students develop disciplinary understandings of narrative writing, the concept of genre, and to develop practices associated with literary writing, such as attention to character development, for example. Within history, students might learn to make sense of primary source documents related to a time period, generate historical interpretations, contextual a character within a particular historical time frame, and consider how a character's particular circumstances might affect how she tells her story.

CREATING A WORK OF HISTORICAL FICTION

	English	*History*
Uses concepts, intellectual tools, frameworks, from at least one discipline	• Concept of narrative writing • Concept of genre • Definition of historical fiction	• Knowledge of a historical period or actors • Historical perspective
Engages students in disciplinary practices	• Developing character and plot in narrative fiction • Revising in response to feedback	• Historical thinking skills, including sourcing and contextualization • Writing a historical narrative

All of the practices noted earlier apply also to interdisciplinary work, although in this case, teachers must work to make sure that the thinking skills, content, and disciplinary practices for both subject areas are visible in the project-related work and assessments. Doing so isn't easy. All too often in interdisciplinary work, one content area can begin to dominate the others, reducing a rich interdisciplinary learning opportunity to a single discipline.[5] For example, in the project related to historical fiction, a teacher might focus entirely on the historical period and pay little attention to the development of narrative understanding and skill. Alternatively, teachers could ask students to focus their attention on the craft of writing—the development of plot, character, and voice—without much attention to historical knowledge, which may lead to well-written, lively, ahistorical accounts. Engaging in multidisciplinary work requires that teachers track the development of disciplinary goals across multiple content areas from project design through project completion.

As we noted previously, it is also all too easy for projects to slip into nondisciplinary goals, as the goal becomes the completion of an engaging project rather than the cultivation of disciplinary knowledge and practice. We could imagine a scenario in which students are asked to produce a work of historical fiction as the culminating project without any instructional attention to either discipline, for example. Another example involves the classic toothpick bridge project. This project could involve significant engagement with subjects like physics (considering the ways that force acts on stationary objects) and history (examining the evolution of bridge design over time). But the project itself could easily be completed without this engagement with the disciplines. Certainly, the students can still learn important things through trial and error, but the disciplinary promise of the project—the opportunity to leverage authentic engagement and excitement of the students to deepen disciplinary understanding—is lost. To ensure that the students deepen their disciplinary understanding, the teacher must identify, construct, and manage components of the project such that they require students to engage with the project through that disciplinary lens. When a bridge falls, the teacher must be prepared to step in and facilitate a conversation that challenges the students to describe this failure in the language of physics and leverage that knowledge to improve their design.

Demands on Teachers' Subject Matter Knowledge

At this point it should be clear that this project-based learning approach requires teachers themselves to have rich disciplinary knowledge if they are to successfully provide these opportunities to students. In the original scenario on the mathematical model for passing time, for example, Ms. Lopez needed to have an understanding of what it means to construct a mathematical model, which approaches to model building are likely to be most constructive, and how to use data to test a model. She also needs a rich repertoire of ways to support students in constructing models themselves, a sense of some of the challenges they might face, and an understanding of some of the predictable misconceptions they might hold—what researchers have called pedagogical content knowledge.[6]

Curriculum designers have long realized the demands that project-based curricula place on teachers' subject matter knowledge. In the 1960s and '70s, rigorous curricula such as Man: A Course of Study, inspired by the work of Jerome Bruner, and Project Physics, developed at Harvard, included projects and investigations as part of the student experiences.[7] This was also the era of the School Mathematics Study Group (SMSG), which developed what is popularly known as "the new math" featuring mathematical concepts and problem solving that left many parents befuddled. The designers were so concerned about the demands on teachers' knowledge in teaching these classes that they attempted to design "teacher-proof curricula," a term that quickly was derided as oxymoronic. As Jerome Bruner himself noted:

> A curriculum is more for teachers than it is for pupils. If it cannot change, move, perturb, inform teachers, it will have no effect on those whom they teach. It must be first and foremost a curriculum for teachers. If it has any effect on pupils, it will have it by virtue of having had an effect on teachers. The doctrine that a well-wrought curriculum is a way of "teacher-proofing" a body of knowledge in order to get it to the student uncontaminated is nonsense.[8]

No matter how rich the curriculum, we need teachers who actually understand the material and teaching/learning well enough to facilitate learning. For these ideas to succeed, we need to invest in teacher development about the complex content we want the students to learn. Teachers also need opportunities to engage in disciplinary practices themselves, to build the muscle memory of what it takes to build a mathematical model, puzzle through a poem, craft a scientific argument. One of the brilliant design features of the National Writing Project was to center the practice of writing right alongside the practice of teaching writing. Other professional development efforts have similarly engaged teachers in ongoing learning of the content alongside learning new ways to teach the content. Project-based learning provides ongoing opportunities for teachers to continue engaging in rich disciplinary learning across their careers, as they explore the questions that are embedded in both disciplinary and interdisciplinary projects.

CONCLUSION

We've begun with disciplinary goals because we see them as a starting point for all project-based learning. Starting with content helps preserve the potential of PBL to create intellectually rich learning experiences for students, in which they have the opportunity to develop disciplinary knowledge, understanding, and tools that will prepare them for future learning. Even though teachers might introduce content knowledge and disciplinary practices in a variety of ways, the goal is that students develop these disciplinary resources *through* working on the project itself. They're using the content and practicing tools of the disciplines as an integral part of their work, and the final project makes visible how they've used those resources. Of course, they're also learning many other things along the way, such as how to work with others, how to communicate with multiple audiences, how to monitor their own learning, how to persist in the face of challenges—all important learning goals for students of all ages. The power to keep on learning, however, rests in large part, on students' opportunities to develop the knowledge, skills, and practices that enable them to go deeper and further in their explorations of the world.

— THREE —

Making It Authentic

*Practices That Support Authentic
Projects and Audiences*

The leaves crunch under the shoes of Ms. Kim and her twenty-seven ninth-grade Earth Science students as they march through the woods behind their school. On this crisp fall day, the students are taking the next step in their water quality project. They have been assigned to prepare a report for the city council about the health of local streams and what their findings add to the lively, and contentious, community conversation regarding the expansion of a local mall. The mall expansion will involve the destruction of an area of wetlands adjacent to a local reservoir that serves both as the community's primary source of drinking water and a major recreation area.

The students' enthusiasm and excitement are palpable as they walk to the creek behind the school, despite a few complaints about the possibility of getting their shoes dirty. While the students have studied the metrics for assessing water quality and performed lab-based water quality tests in their classroom, this is their first opportunity to use their new knowledge and skills in a setting outside the classroom. Of course, this setting creates a few challenges for Ms. Kim as she tries to maintain some order in this high-energy group, but she is willing to make that trade-off because this is also a great opportunity to emphasize the authentic nature of the project; the scientific data that students produce will contribute to a real conversation around a real problem in their community.

As the students arrive at the site, Ms. Kim gathers them for a brief set of reminders and instructions about how to use the next thirty minutes. She begins by highlighting the purpose of their trip to the stream—to practice collecting data and interpreting the results of that data in order to contribute to the larger community discussion about the potential impacts of expanding the mall on the water quality in their community. After a few reminders about the roles assigned to members of each group, she sends them off to find different sites to collect samples.

As one of the groups begins to set up equipment to test for levels of nitrates in the water, Ms. Kim recognizes an opportunity to check students' understanding. She asks, "Remind me, why is it that an environmental scientist might care about the level of nitrates in the water?" Paul, the jokester of the group, immediately jumps in: "They don't! They are too busy saving the pandas!" Ms. Kim gives him her patented "teacher look" raised eyebrow. There is the inevitable pause as the students eye one another to see who is willing to venture a real answer before Antoine offers a suggestion: "Well, nitrates are food for algae? Right?" There's a pause, as the students all look to Ms. Kim for confirmation. When it's clear that she is, in turn, waiting on them, Alice replies, "No, I think the nitrates poison fish." Ms. Kim sees the need to address a misperception and chimes in at this point, "Well, they don't actually poison the fish, but they can contribute to the death of fish. Antoine was on to something. Nitrates *are* food for algae, but so what? Why might that be a problem?" Alice thinks for a moment before responding, "Ah, I remember! If there is too much food, it can create an algal bloom. . . ."

Ms. Kim turns now to Juan, who she knows is an avid fisherman and has been vigorously waving his hand to get her attention. "Juan, ever had any problems with algal blooms around here?" Juan launches into an animated story about how his favorite fishing spot was ruined last summer after an algal bloom lowered the levels of oxygen in the water and forced all of the fish to leave that area. Ms. Kim listens to his explanation for a bit but then decides it is time to move the group on; she knows they could get completely sidetracked in his story and miss the opportunity to gather the necessary data. "OK, I think we see how this was a problem. So, let's get back to testing that water! And I'll leave you with this question: could the mall expansion cause any problems with additional nitrates? Is this something we should be concerned about in our report to the city council?" As Ms. Kim moves on to the next group, she is pleased to hear the group launching into a debate about the importance of nitrate levels in relation to the planned expansion of the mall.

AUTHENTICITY

The project that Ms. Kim is leading asks students to learn about issues in the local community and use their knowledge of environmental science to directly contribute to an ongoing debate. This exercise demands that they think about the issues from the perspective of both scientists and members of the community. They also have significant opportunities to think about why and how this debate is meaningful in their own lives. These opportunities to do real work, make a real impact, and feel a personal connection to the work all support the creation of an authentic learning experience for the students.

Educators often describe projects like the one Ms. Kim was leading as "authentic." When teachers talk about authenticity in the classroom context, they are frequently referring to the alignment between what is done in the classroom and what people do in the real world. Activities, projects, and tasks in a science classroom that more closely resemble the work that scientists actually do are more authentic than a classroom where students spend all of their time memorizing facts. Take, for instance, one of the learning goals in the sample environmental science unit: cultivating students' capacity to assess the health of a body of water. This goal could be accomplished by requiring students to memorize common pollutants, their sources, and the environmental impacts of each pollutant. Certainly, environmental scientists need this knowledge, but memorizing these facts looks very little like what environmental scientists do day-to-day. The work toward this goal can be made more authentic through a project in which students actually test the quality of a local body of water. This task requires that they not just know the pollutants, sources, and their impacts but actually put this knowledge into action to synthesize the data they gather and evaluate the quality of an actual body of water—an activity that more closely resembles the work of environmental scientists in state and local organizations that monitor water quality.

Just doing the things that environmental scientists do is only one component of how teachers build authenticity in PBL projects. If the work that students do is entirely contained within the school walls, the authenticity of those tasks may be limited. Which of these is more authentic: taking the results of the water quality analysis project and producing a lab report that constitutes a major grade *or* conducting the testing as a part of a project in coordination with a local environmental group that will take all of the student reports and aggregate them into a larger report to be submitted to the local city or town council? Clearly, the opportunity to make a contribution beyond the classroom walls, the opportunity for the student work to have an impact on local policy and be useful to a local organization, can take a project to an enhanced level of authenticity.

For some teachers, authentic activity is not just doing things that are similar to what scientists do and that make an impact beyond school walls. A learning experience can do both of these things and still feel disconnected for students. A final component of authenticity is the personal connections that students have or build with the work. This component is different from motivation. Rather, it is if the students actually see themselves in that work. This connection might come naturally based on the students' prior interests or might be something that the teacher has to build by helping students see how they are personally connected to the work. In the water quality unit, some students might feel personally connected to the work because of their experience fishing or swimming at the local lake. But the teacher might also build these personal connections by helping the students understand how the water that comes out of the tap at their house comes directly from that lake.

Together, these three components of authenticity are what we hear teachers talk about when they describe their goal of building authentic experiences for students. They seek to build experiences that correlate with the work of professionals in the field, that have an impact beyond the school, and that are meaningful to students. It should be noted that not all teachers think about authenticity in all three ways; some may emphasize certain dimensions over others. It is also important to note that a project is not simply authentic or inauthentic. We think that authenticity exists on a spectrum and projects can be more or less authentic along different dimensions depending on how teachers engage with the three components of authenticity we have identified. Consequently, teachers don't have to create a perfectly authentic project across all three of these dimensions. Instead, we encourage educators to consider what changes can be made, both in planning and implementation, that will push students' experiences further along these dimensions of authenticity. In support of that effort, we have identified three core practices related to authenticity—one for each of the components of authenticity identified here. (See figure 3.1.)

CORE PRACTICE
SUPPORT STUDENTS TO MAKE A
CONTRIBUTION TO THE WORLD

Many educators perceive their role as preparing students for their future lives. While this is without question an important role for educators, it is also a limited one. Teachers who believe that students have the capacity to make meaningful contributions to the world don't wait for the future; they create opportunities for students to explore what they are capable of contributing in the here and now.

Some teachers talk about this way of thinking as having a focus on real problems or a connection to the real world. We believe real problems are those that extend beyond the particular assignment. They are real in

FIGURE 3.1   Authentic practice

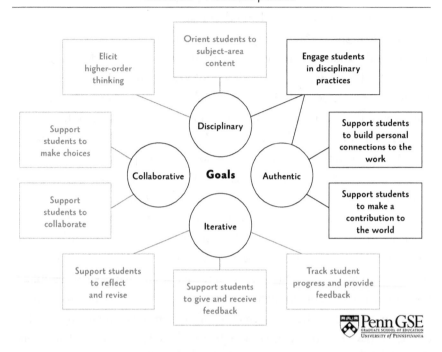

Source: Pam Grossman, Christopher Pupik Dean, Sarah Schneider Kavanagh, and Zachary Herrmann. "Preparing Teachers for Project-Based Teaching." kappanonline.org, March 25, 2019. https:// kappanonline.org/preparing-teachers-project-based-teaching-grossman-pupik-dean-kavanagh-herrmann/.

that they are not just problems because a teacher has identified them as such (by assigning a problem set, for example), but because others (students, a community, or an academic discipline) have identified them as such. See the "Making a Contribution and a Connection to the World " chart, which identifies a few examples of activities that students might engage in at school that either do or do not allow students to engage in these real problems and make a contribution to the communities where these problems exist.

In deeply authentic classrooms, it can feel like there are no walls between the classroom and the world around it. This level of authenticity

MAKING A CONTRIBUTION AND A CONNECTION TO THE WORLD

Limited contribution/connection to the world	Significant contribution/connection to the world
• Memorizing scientific facts and reproducing those facts for the purpose of a test • Writing an essay about a book for the teacher to read and evaluate • Successfully completing a mathematical proof of a claim the teacher provided • Preparing a slide presentation for the class that summarizes the events that led to WWI	• Designing and running a scientific experiment on water quality and sharing the results with the city council • Creating a critical review of a book and submitting it for publication in the student newspaper • Using real traffic data to create a mathematical model and present it to city planners • Researching the impacts of "soda taxes," developing a position on the topic, and then advocating that position in an op-ed

may feel difficult for many teachers to accomplish. The good news is that we can all take smaller steps toward deep authenticity by creating opportunities for students to engage with the problems, goals, and questions of a variety of communities both within and outside the classroom. This means that the students might be exploring a challenge for their local community or a virtual community. For many students in many classrooms, the sole audience for their work is the teacher. However, if we hope to support our students to make a contribution to the world, we need to rethink who can be the audience for their work.

While teachers might support students to make a contribution to the world in a number of ways, we have seen three primary strategies: drawing examples from communities, connecting classroom activities to the problems and challenges of communities, and creating opportunities to present to audiences drawn from communities or audiences that approximate communities.

Creating Authentic Examples

One of the easiest ways that a teacher might support students to connect with communities beyond the classroom is through the use of examples drawn from real contexts outside the classroom that can be used to illustrate concepts and knowledge that are a focus of the project. By bringing real examples into the classroom, the teacher can help students connect the concepts they are learning in school with questions, problems, or opportunities that exist in the broader world. In the vignette that opened this chapter, Ms. Kim drew her student, Juan, into the conversation to provide a concrete example from his own experience.

♦ IDEAS TO TRY

Set a goal of having at least one example drawn from real contexts per lesson.

This example was grounded not only in Juan's personal experience but also in the fishing community that relies on the lake for recreation. Teachers might also use video clips and text drawn from sources that the students are familiar with as illustrations of these ideas. You might also find a teacher drawing on current events or recent past events as a means of linking students to events beyond the school walls. Ms. Kim, by engaging the students around a topic that was an active discussion in their community, will have significant local resources to draw on, but she might also engage examples from outside that community to illustrate the relevance of this issue to other communities. Drawing these connections can encourage students to make links between course content and the broader world. As we see in the vignette, PBL practitioners need to be able to identify relevant examples and to draw them in and deploy them in the classroom at the appropriate time. Ms. Kim had to have the knowledge of Juan's background in fishing and call him into the conversation at the right time to be able to make this connection. Note that she could have just approached this group and simply told them why nitrates were important to consider. Instead, she supported them to move toward the answer on their own and through examples drawn from their own experience.

Exploring Authentic Problems

Teachers who are seeking to build authentic learning opportunities can also make frequent connections to the real challenges and problems faced by communities that care about the issues the class is examining. While teachers might use an example of a real problem to illustrate a point, some teachers take the next step to use this problem to frame the larger project.

For example, Ms. Kim framed the purpose and final product of the water quality project around an ongoing debate in the local community and throughout that project was then able to point to that debate as an answer to the inevitable questions from students: "Why are we doing this? When are

♦ **IDEAS TO TRY**

When planning your project, identify a community for whom the project really matters.

we ever going to use this knowledge?" Of course, it will not be possible to always have such a debate going on in a teacher's local community, so PBL teachers may have to identify the most relevant communities that are actually facing the problem that is the focus of that project. Often one is closer than might be expected! As noted previously, engaging in this practice involves more than just identifying these problems and contexts.

Teachers also have to know when and how to remind students of these problems. In our work, we have seen teachers use introductions and reminders at the beginning and the end of a class. We have also seen teachers make more nuanced moves to frame questions to students in ways that require them to consider their work through the lens of the problem being addressed. In our vignette, Ms. Kim makes such a move in her last comment to the group of students, asking them to consider their renewed understanding of nitrates in relation to the proposed expansion of the local mall.

Engaging Authentic Audience

Teachers creating authentic spaces also rely on real audiences to build an authentic experience for students. In many classrooms, the only audience for students' work is the teacher. This is not the case in many classrooms that strive for higher levels of authenticity. These teachers draw on real examples, frame projects around real problems, and then find an audience for the student work that is actively considering those problems. (See "Getting Started with Supporting Students to Make a Contribution to the World: Questions to Ask Yourself.") In Ms. Kim's case, this authentic audience is the local city council. It is not the only audience that she might have engaged. She could have required students to submit an op-ed to the local paper or make a presentation to parents or other students in their school to inform them about the potential concerns with the local mall expansion; she also might have provided them with the option of presenting to any of these audiences. Leveraging an authentic audience not only reminds students of the particular problems they are trying to address in the real world but also orients students to how others will receive their final product, solutions, arguments, or presentations. With the city council as the audience, Ms. Kim can now ask students to consider their work through the eyes of that audience: What does the city council need to know? What arguments and information will be compelling? This approach allows the teacher to make frequent references to the audience as she supports students to consider what should be included in their project and how that content should be presented.

CORE PRACTICE
ENGAGE STUDENTS IN DISCIPLINARY PRACTICES

As noted in the previous chapter, engaging students in disciplinary practices focuses on supporting students to take on those disciplinary problems in a particular way—one that is authentic to the discipline or field that is the subject of the course. In a math course, this approach means supporting students to think, talk, and problem-solve like mathematicians. In a STEM course, it may mean supporting students to think, talk, and problem-solve like engineers. In a writing course, it may mean supporting students to think, talk, and problem-solve like journalists. In this chapter, we explore how teachers create this engagement in disciplinary practices and how it contributes to the authenticity of project-based learning.

We have observed teachers engaging students in disciplinary practices through two primary strategies. The first involves engaging students in disciplinary inquiry, where students explore a problem that is actively being examined within the discipline. Second, we see teachers supporting students to engage in disciplinary talk, where students are supported to use the language, tools, and processes of the discipline.

Disciplinary Inquiry

To support students to engage in disciplinary inquiry, teachers have to be familiar with the problems that disciplinarians are working on and set up projects in ways that engage students around those problems. This approach first involves knowing the disciplinary problems. The PBL teachers we have worked with often cite their continued engagement in their discipline—for example, reading current work in academic journals or partnering with academic researchers in summer projects at a local university. These teachers then work to translate the disciplinary problems that are currently being examined in the field into projects that are appropriate for their students' level of experience and course learning goals. However, situating the larger project in disciplinary problems is necessary but not sufficient for engaging students in disciplinary inquiry. Throughout these projects, the teacher must actively support students to engage in this inquiry by reminding them of the disciplinary nature of the project.

One strategy we have seen employed to support students in this way is simply asking the question, "How would an environmental scientist (or historian or mathematician or journalist) think about this particular problem?" Ms. Kim does just this as she first approaches the group of students in the vignette. She does not just ask what problem nitrates might cause in a stream but explicitly frames her question through the lens of an environmental scientist. By asking this question, she reminds students to consider the professionals in the field who engage in analogous work. Students are then supported to employ the same processes, techniques, and technologies that professionals in the fields use, thus making the disciplinary work all the more authentic. Environmental scientists measure the quality of water using the same metrics as those being employed by Ms. Kim's class, allowing her the opportunity to bring in actual reports from environmental scientists who have done similar work and use those as examples. She might also be able to invite environmental scientists from a local university or state office to speak with her class about how they approach these problems in their own work.

Disciplinary Talk

A large part of what disciplinary scholars do is to communicate with one another about the discipline. In addition to PBL teachers framing student work around disciplinary problems and practices of the discipline or field, we have observed them engaging students in disciplinary practices by supporting students to discuss, converse, debate, argue, and critique in ways that are authentic to the discipline. Ms. Kim's entire interaction with the students in the opening vignette supported this sort of talk. She initiated a conversation around a question of disciplinary significance and did not lecture the students about it but provided the scaffolds and supports necessary to help the students engage in that talk. In more traditional classrooms, we might see teachers engaging in most of the disciplinary talk, but in this case, Ms. Kim stepped in only when she thought it necessary to correct a misconception; the rest of the time she was putting the onus on the students to engage in that talk. This support of disciplinary talk extends into other forms of communication such as written reports and presentations. In this way, teachers build the students' capacity to engage in the work using vocabulary and modes of expression that are used within these disciplines, enhancing their capacity to participate in those discourses. (See chapter 2 to explore how to get started with engaging students in disciplinary practices.)

CORE PRACTICE
HELP STUDENTS BUILD PERSONAL
CONNECTIONS TO THE WORK

The chasm between school and self is indefensibly large for far too many students. It is also the case that this disconnection is largest for our most disadvantaged students. When students do not have the opportunity to see themselves within their work at school, they may struggle to make the connections between their academic work and self that can support their development as critical and life-long learners. Rather than school representing a space disconnected from their lives, it should be a place for students to more fully explore and develop themselves, including as it relates to their cultural heritage and lived experiences. School can be a powerful forum for young people to draw on their experiences, culture, values, perspectives, and beliefs, as well as have those aspects of themselves challenged and developed. (See "Personal Connections.")

To support students to cultivate meaning in their work, teachers may attempt to link the project to students' interests or help the students learn how they might be connected to the content of the project. We have seen teachers engage in this practice through three main strategies. First,

PERSONAL CONNECTIONS

A lack of personal connections	Powerful personal connections
• Students' experiences, values, perspectives, and beliefs have little or nothing to do with the learning experience.	• Students' experiences, values, perspectives, and beliefs represent critical assets for a project, making the experience richer and more whole.
• Students are provided with examples that are drawn from contexts that are not culturally relevant.	• Teachers use examples that are culturally relevant and culturally sustaining.[1]
• Students are assigned novels that are not connected with their own experiences.	• Students are assigned novels that both do and do not connect to their own experiences, but the teacher engages in activities to support development of empathy.
• Students complete decontextualized mathematical problem sets.	• Mathematical problem sets are contextualized according to their application in the world.

teachers use student interests and local contacts to generate examples that contextualize the content of a project. Second, teachers find ways to amplify students' voices and autonomy through their work on the project. Finally, teachers spend time making explicit connections between the project, project goals, and student interests and goals. Learning about students is central to this practice. Teachers utilizing project-based learning must develop relationships with students that allow them to understand what motivates them, what experiences they bring with them, and what their interests are. Some teachers develop surveys to learn about student interests at the beginning of the academic year, but we saw many project-based teachers dedicating small but significant amounts of time at the opening and end of classes to building community, such as taking five minutes at the beginning of a class to provide a forum for students to share exciting news with their classmates. Making these connections not only helps teachers build an understanding of what students care about but also builds that understanding in a community of peers. (See "Getting Started with Helping Students Build Personal Connections to the Work: Questions to Ask Yourself.")

♦ IDEAS TO TRY

Dedicate five minutes at the start of each class to community-building activities.

Getting Started with Helping Students Build Personal Connections to the Work:
QUESTIONS TO ASK YOURSELF

Getting to know students:

- How do I collect information about students' experiences and interests?
- How might I utilize that information to inform project planning and implementation?
- How might students' experiences and ideas serve as a resource for themselves and for each other?

Acknowledging student voice:

- Where, within the project, are there opportunities for students to draw on their own experiences, preferences, or values?

Reflecting on a lesson:

- Were the examples I used in class today directly relatable to the students in my classroom?
- Were there missed opportunities to encourage students to take ownership of the work?

Relevant Examples

As teachers work to build authentic classrooms, they spend significant time trying to make the content meaningful for students by drawing examples from students' interests. By situating a project within contexts that are familiar or relevant to students, teachers can help students see meaning in the project. In a way, Ms. Kim's entire project creates a relevant example because it is so deeply connected to an ongoing debate in the local community. But she also relies on this strategy when making the connections to Juan's experience as an avid angler. Clearly, this effort requires that the teacher spend time getting to know her students and their interests outside school so that she can draw on these examples as the need arises. In English classrooms, teachers use tools like anticipation guides that prepare students for reading texts by asking them to consider their own attitudes and opinions about topics in that text. Another common strategy is a simple reflective journal completed at the end of a class that includes prompts that provide students with the opportunity to synthesize their learning and generate connections to the things that they care about.

Cultivating Student Voice

In addition to identifying examples that might have meaning for students, many accomplished PBL teachers spend significant time encouraging students' voices within projects. These teachers see the encouragement of student voice as critical to supporting students to make connections to the project—working under the idea that increased agency and control over the project allows the students to bring more of themselves into the work. Enabling student voice first requires that projects be set up in a way that allows students to make choices. However, simply creating the opportunity for students to make choices is often not sufficient to truly cultivate their voice. Teachers must actively encourage students to engage in opportunities for choice and voice. Unfortunately, school is often a place where students get little choice. As a result, students have been enculturated in a system where they primarily look to follow their teachers' guidance rather than engage their own ideas. Teachers have to actively support students to unlearn this tendency. Doing so is deceptively simple and extremely difficult at the same time.

♦ IDEAS TO TRY

Examine your projects to find new ways to give students more (and more significant) choices about their work.

One way that teachers can cultivate student choice is by highlighting how students have made similar choices in the past—for example, by illustrating to students the significant and meaningful choices previous students have made by showing the class exemplar projects that reflect a diverse set of choices made by students. Teachers can encourage students to consider how their own voice would come into these projects and how the exemplar projects illustrate the choices that previous students made.

While the most obvious opportunities to support student choice come at the beginning of a project when students are selecting a topic and strategy to approach it, opportunities to encourage student voice occur all the time. These opportunities often present themselves when teachers engage in consultation with a group of students. In these situations, teachers are often asked their opinion on an idea or choice a student is making. It can be easy for teachers to simply answer the student and provide a suggestion, but teachers interested in supporting student voice often pause before making such suggestions. We see Ms. Kim making such a pause as all of the students look to her to affirm a student's suggestion. While teachers often step in at these moments, Ms. Kim holds back and steps in only after she sees that a misconception must be addressed. Instead of accomplished PBL teachers answering these questions, we have seen them turn the question back on the student and emphasize the student's agency in determining the path forward. This focus on student agency supports students to make the project their own rather than work they are merely doing for their teachers.

Making Explicit Links

Finally, teachers draw on their knowledge of students to make links between the students' interests outside the classroom and the projects they work on within the classroom. Students do not always see these connections on their own. A version of this strategy involves bringing in certain students as experts, as Ms. Kim did in the vignette that opens this chapter. When a teacher knows that a student has a specialized interest, experience, or expertise in a given area, this knowledge allows her to center the student as an expert to the class or group. Centering a student can also demonstrate to other students how the project can be important to people outside the classroom even if it is not directly important to them.

CONCLUSION

Authenticity is a critical component of project-based learning. We are certainly not the first to identify the importance of creating authentic experiences for students in project-based classrooms. Examples can be seen in the existing frameworks and literature on project-based learning.[2] But what we hope we have helped to illuminate is the many ways that project-based teachers think about and work to cultivate authenticity in their classrooms. We know that creating classrooms where students do real work, make a real impact, and feel connected to their work can seem challenging, but as with all of the practices described in this book, movement toward that ultimate goal is something that happens over an extended period of time as teachers experiment, explore, and reflect on their work with students. Following are a few strategies we have heard teachers using to move themselves toward more authentic classrooms.

First, get to know your local context. As we have seen, drawing connections between student interests and the communities around them—including disciplinary communities—is central to the practice of developing authentic classrooms. This effort requires teachers to know their community, as well as their discipline. The teachers we have interacted with talk about the work they do to continue developing their understanding of their discipline, make connections within their community, and develop a deeper understanding of the interests of their students.

Second, pay attention to the local, national, and international news. Current events can play a significant role in supporting teachers' capacity to make connections to the communities outside the classroom and to student interests. Teachers we spoke with spent time understanding events of the day, not just those that relate to their own interests, but also to those of their students and to their disciplines and fields. The school newspaper is another media source that allows teachers to draw connections between classroom activity and broader school activities, such as the school's new dress code, the nutritional value of meals offered at lunch, or the latest performance of the chess club or the soccer team. These activities can provide easily accessible examples for students to make connections between what they are learning in class and the problems and opportunities in their school community.

Finally, consider playing the "authenticity game." You can explore the authenticity of your own work with colleagues by presenting a project, classroom activity, or lesson and collectively exploring strategies to make the learning experience one step more authentic. Remember, authenticity exists on a continuum, and our own team of authors has found it both enjoyable and productive to explore the ideas of authenticity in this way. Simply take an idea for a learning experience and ask what makes it authentic, what would make it more authentic, and what would make it less authentic? It's amazing how far these questions can take you in exploring the concept of authenticity, which will allow you to develop a deeper understanding of what is important to you in creating authentic experiences for your students.

— F O U R —

Learning to Collaborate

*Practices That Build Student Agency
in Learning Communities*

"What are the chances? Can you believe it?!" yells Mr. Singer over the raucous cheers of his students. The class stares at the quarter that lies heads-up on the floor. It's the fifth heads in a row. "How long can this go on?" Mr. Singer eggs on his students. Zoraya, a seventh-grade student, yells out, "I bet you anything the next flip will be tails. It's got to be!" Mr. Singer takes advantage of the moment to hit pause on the coin flips. Lowering his voice to draw in his students' attention, Mr. Singer asks, "Zoraya thinks the next flip will be tails. By a show of hands, who agrees with her?"

Several hands shoot up. Other students seem visibly frustrated by the question, unable to share the complexity of their thoughts by merely "agreeing" or "disagreeing." Mr. Singer then asks his class who disagrees. Some hands stay up, others come down. A few students appear eager to speak up. "Okay, I want you to turn to your group and discuss: what do you think the next coin flip will be. I don't just want to hear your answer; I want to hear your *argument*."

Students quickly turn to face their groups, and Mr. Singer begins walking his slow lap around the classroom. The energy (and volume) of the first group he passes is intense. Students talk over each other as they each try to make their point. Mr. Singer pauses for a moment and then asks, "Who is the facilitator in this group?" Sarah raises her hand. "Sarah, can you please make sure everyone has a chance to share their thoughts? It seems like your team members have quite a bit to say! It would be a shame if your group didn't have an opportunity to benefit from everyone's ideas."

As Mr. Singer walks on, he notices the group in the back of the classroom. In stark contrast to the first group, this group's members sit in silence. As Mr. Singer approaches, he notices a few thoughts scribbled on Andre's notebook. "Andre, it looks like you have some important ideas to share with your team. Can you please make sure your team has an opportunity to hear them?" The team members turn to Andre, as Mr. Singer walks on.

After two minutes of students talking in their groups, Mr. Singer calls students' attention back to the front of the classroom. After the class is polled, it's clear that there is great disagreement about what students can predict regarding the next coin flip. A third of the class asserts that there's a 50/50 chance the flip will be tails, while two-thirds of the class think that it's far more likely than 50/50, given that a tail is "long overdue."

"A coin flip is an example of what we call a random event. What are other examples of random events?" After a short pause, students start shouting out ideas, as Mr. Singer documents them on the board. Mr. Singer captures a dozen student responses and then turns back to the class. When Marcus starts to plead with Mr. Singer to "flip the coin, already," Mr. Singer decides to leverage the class's rapt attention. "We will flip the coin again, in just a moment . . . but first, I need to tell you about why we even started flipping it in the first place. We're about to launch into a team project."

"As a team, you're going to make a choice regarding a topic you want to explore. While making a choice as an individual can be difficult, making a choice as a team can pose even more challenges. What are some ways teams can make choices?" One student raises her hand and suggests that the team could vote. Another student says, "The team should just talk about it and decide together." Mr. Singer probes further, asking what would happen if the students within the team couldn't come to a collective agreement. Another student offers "majority rules!" Students continue to offer suggestions until one student suggests that the team could flip a coin. Immediately, another student yells, "It's going to be tails!" and the class erupts in laughter.

"In a minute, you will work as a group to pick a topic your group will explore. Ultimately, your task will be to use your understanding of probability to determine what we know about the likelihood of your topic, the misconceptions that may exist, and to communicate your findings to an appropriate audience, given your topic." Mr. Singer hands out the project description and rubric.

"This project will require your group to draw on a variety of mathematical concepts, as well as utilize a variety of skills from your team members. This project will require you to use random data sets, create probability models, construct viable mathematical arguments, and compute expected values. This project will also require you to communicate complex ideas in ways that are accessible to broad audiences, negotiate different preferences within your group, and draw on the experiences and creative insights of your team members. For your group to be successful, you will need to find ways to draw on the knowledge and insights from every member of your group."

"Process managers, please raise your hand. Process managers—remember, take the final five minutes of today's class to debrief your process, evaluate your progress, and establish your goals for tomorrow's class session. Be sure to refer to the project timeline in the project description card." Mr. Singer prompts groups to refer back to their team commitments and role assignments, and then asks the student in the "ideation role" to kick off the group's brainstorming process.

COLLABORATION

Mr. Singer's middle school class is embarking on a project that will require students to work together. At times, the mathematical ideas that students will grapple with will offer significant challenges for students, pushing and stretching them in productive ways as learners. By working together, students stand to benefit from the unique insights, perspectives, ideas, and creativity of their peers. In essence, that is the promise of collaboration: when it is done effectively, students are able to take on more complex work, driving to more thoughtful and creative solutions. In Mr. Singer's classroom, students will dive into bigger and more significant mathematical questions as a team compared to what they could do alone.

However, the math will surely not be the only source of productive struggle. Without a doubt, through the process of working together, students will be challenged by the demands of collaboration. They will struggle to make collective decisions. They will struggle to draw on the insights of all their team members. They will struggle with interpersonal challenges. And they will struggle with assigning roles, delegating tasks, holding each other accountable, monitoring their progress, and learning from their mistakes. For many teachers, these struggles can quickly tip the scale on whether or not having students collaborate is even worthwhile in the first place.

For Mr. Singer, the decision of whether or not to have his students collaborate isn't as simple as a definitive "yes" or "no." For him, the questions focus on *when* it makes sense to have his students collaborate, and the level of support and scaffolds he needs to provide to help ensure that the collaboration is productive. Mr. Singer recognizes that collaboration is most useful for certain projects and less useful for others. Projects that are open-ended, are complex, and require a diverse set of skills such as creativity, problem-solving, and communication are best for collaboration because individual students are not likely to be successful on their own. For these types of projects to work, students must draw the knowledge and skills of multiple students. This is not to say, however, that all projects must be collaborative ones. In plenty of individual projects students are able to pursue their own unique interests and passions on their own. Even so, because developing collaborative capacity is a central goal for most project-based educators, creating ample opportunities for students to collaborate—and providing the support for them to do so effectively—is central to the work of project-based learning teachers.

Mr. Singer knows that students may be able to develop far deeper insights and understandings when they work together on the probability project. The project lends itself to benefiting from students working, exploring, and solving problems together. However, just because collaboration offers more ambitious possibilities doesn't mean that those possibilities are always realized. For collaboration to work, Mr. Singer implements a series of intentional supports and interventions, some preplanned and some responsive in the moment, to support students to effectively make choices and collaborate. Beyond the math that Mr. Singer hopes his students will learn, he also has explicit goals to develop his students' ability to make thoughtful choices and collaborate effectively. (See figure 4.1.)

Making Real Choices

Beyond the rich disciplinary learning that can occur in thoughtfully designed and executed projects, teachers who utilize project-based learning often cite cultivating student agency and ownership as a fundamental benefit of the project-based learning approach. PBL teachers spend time thoughtfully considering where and how students will have opportunities within a project to make decisions of consequence—decisions that shape their own experiences. These decisions can range in focus from project goals to project process to the questions surrounding the classroom learning environment.

Working Together

Project-based learning also creates opportunities for students to develop their skills in working with other students on complex and meaningful work, over extended periods of time, toward collective goals. Rather than seeing their classmates merely as resources to pursue individual goals, or—in some cases—as competitors in a climate of competition and scarcity, students can see their classmates as integral members of a collective learning community. As members of a learning community, students can experience the benefits and challenges of balancing individual and collective goals, and the possibilities that exist when people come together to take on complex and meaningful work.

FIGURE 4.1   Collaborative domain

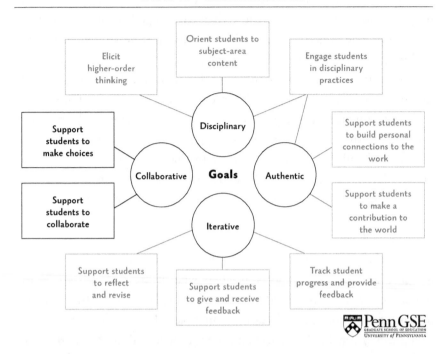

Source: Pam Grossman, Christopher Pupik Dean, Sarah Schneider Kavanagh, and Zachary Herrmann. "Preparing Teachers for Project-Based Teaching." kappanonline.org, March 25, 2019. https://kappanonline.org/preparing-teachers-project-based-teaching-grossman-pupik-dean-kavanagh-herrmann/.

CORE PRACTICE
SUPPORT STUDENTS TO MAKE CHOICES

Many educators hope to build their students' confidence, agency, and ownership over their learning. Unfortunately, these hopes are undermined by the prescriptive nature of most learning experiences. More often than not, students are directed on what to do and how to do it. Without opportunities for students to make significant choices, imagining how they might develop their individual sense of purpose and efficacy is difficult. Furthermore, the challenges facing our society require individuals who are able to balance individual interests with shared goals, and at times, even negotiating the very nature and direction of those shared goals. Many teachers find that project-based learning can create genuine opportunities for students to practice individual and collective decision-making. It should be noted, however, that teachers who embrace student choice typically do not see it as an absolute. For many project aspects, it may make sense for teachers to hold on to their authority to make decisions, such as choices regarding project focus, timeline, overarching learning goals, and key benchmarks. However, that still leaves plenty of opportunities for students to make meaningful decisions. Accomplished PBL teachers work hard to ensure that students have opportunities to make decisions that matter, rather than simply predetermining every aspect of the project without student input. (See "Who Makes the Decisions?")

Supporting Student Choice and Ownership of Learning Community

In spite of some efforts to do so, teachers alone cannot create a learning community by edict. A community is built by the collective actions of all its members, which means that all students must feel ownership over a community and work toward its development and maintenance. In project-based learning classrooms, teachers rely heavily on students to play active roles in community-building work. Mr. Singer does this by creating plenty of opportunities for students to interact with one another, discuss and debate ideas, and learn from each other. However, merely increasing student interaction does not guarantee that a productive community will

WHO MAKES THE DECISIONS?

No decisions of consequence	*Students exercising choice*
• All elements of the project are predetermined by the teacher, including project goals, process, and product. • Students experience only choices that have limited consequence, such as their team's name or the order they deliver their presentation.	• Students have input on some elements of a project, including their personal learning goals, the learning goals of their team, the process they employ, and/or the form of their final product.

develop. As many teachers know all too well, along with increased student interaction can come problematic dynamics that can be detrimental to an inclusive and effective learning community. For example, issues of power, bias, and interpersonal conflict are likely to happen. When students work together, status issues can lead to inequitable participation and opportunities to engage and learn.[1] Therefore, teachers must be careful observers, constantly watching for status issues and intervening when necessary. Furthermore, it's important for teachers to create structured spaces for students to process and reflect on their community and consider the improvements they hope to make.

Before engaging his students in an extended group project, Mr. Singer worked hard to build a strong foundation for collaborative learning. From the first day of school, Mr. Singer engaged his students in short team-building activities that helped develop and reinforce a very particular set of classroom norms. These norms explicitly speak to collaborative behavior, such as "Pay attention to what other group members need" and "No one is done til' everyone is done."[2] For example, instead of activities that valued competition and speed (something quite common in many math classrooms), Mr. Singer's activities required students to cooperate, communicate, discuss, and make choices. Mr. Singer also knew that activities and tasks that always ended in one correct answer might reinforce narrow conceptions of the discipline (e.g., that math is about "getting the right answer") that would eventually be inhibitors for collaboration. Rather than focusing on quickly getting to the right answer, these activities and challenges encouraged creativity, problem solving, and the discovery of multiple methods to solve problems. Because creativity, problem-solving, and discovery can be bolstered when students work together, these activities helped students appreciate what their peers had to offer and gave them experience working together on problems that were less straightforward and routine. Mr. Singer also scaffolded student discussions and interactions, nurturing his students' capacity to work with each other. He started with frequent, yet short, opportunities for students

♦ IDEAS TO TRY

Create a set of norms for students to use while working in small teams.

to engage in think-pair-shares and eventually worked toward longer, more sustained interaction and problem-solving. Over time, students developed both the skills and mindsets that would prepare them for more intense and prolonged opportunities to make choices and collaborate.

Supporting Student Choice and Ownership in Project Goals

Many teachers struggle to find a balance between supporting students to pursue a set of common, predetermined learning goals (sometimes prescribed by policy) on one hand and honoring students' unique preferences and interests on the other hand. However, accomplished project-based learning teachers don't always see this as an either/or choice. Consider the project that Mr. Singer introduces to his class in the opening vignette. Mr. Singer clearly has a set of specific learning goals for his students. He wants all students to use random data sets, create probability models, construct viable mathematical arguments, and compute expected values. However, he also creates space for students to pursue their own interests and goals within their project by allowing them to pick the specific topic that they would like to explore. While all students will engage with the same mathematical practices and use the same mathematical tools, they'll do so by exploring questions that most interest them.

For example, one group of students decides to explore card games, such as poker and blackjack. Another group chooses to investigate their state's lottery game, drawing on the recent hype of the ever-growing jackpot. Another group plans to explore the chances of getting stopped at traffic lights (they blame their "bad luck" for being late to school). Yet another group plans to explore the US Selective Service System, given that they know they are legally obligated to register in just a few years, and they are growing curious about the chances of being "drafted" if a draft were to occur.

Teachers must consider which project and learning goals are foundational to the experience and should be standard across all students. For many classrooms, this consideration will likely entail some of the essential questions, foundational knowledge, and disciplinary practices of the subject. Even when the teacher establishes these goals, students will likely still have a great deal of flexibility to make their own goals related to their project and to their learning, which is possible through the investigation of the questions they choose.

Supporting Student Choice and Ownership in Project Process

While some projects have the potential to offer a great deal of student choice, teachers can overly prescribe the process all too easily. Rather than students building and owning their own process, they are asked to follow a cookbook recipe that has been given to them. Teachers in project-based learning classrooms see the process of working through a project as a valuable learning opportunity in itself. Beyond having to learn how to anticipate and react to challenges, manage resources and time, and make adequate progress toward project benchmarks and goals, giving students more of the responsibility over their own process can help build a sense of ownership over their project. (See "Getting Started with Supporting Students to Make Choices: Questions to Ask Yourself.")

With increased responsibility over the process comes increased demands on students. Many students (let alone adults!) find it difficult to effectively manage the process. Consequently, teachers in project-based classrooms tend to utilize scaffolds and supports to ensure students are prepared to take on this increased responsibility. For example, Mr. Singer uses student roles as one way to support the group process. He also builds in time at the end of each day for all the process managers to facilitate a reflection period with their teams regarding their team process and their progress on the project. Mr. Singer also provides groups with a project timeline, which can help groups understand whether or not they are on track. Even with these universal supports given to all groups, some of Mr. Singer's groups will surely struggle with the responsibility of managing their group process. In such cases, Mr. Singer will likely provide more intensive interventions directed at specific groups, such as facilitating group reflections himself, providing more structure for how the group spends its time, building in more

♦ **IDEAS TO TRY**

Have students assume specific roles while working in small teams.

> ## Getting Started with Supporting Students to Make Choices:
> ## QUESTIONS TO ASK YOURSELF
>
> In thinking about an upcoming project (or unit), consider the following questions:
>
> Learning community:
>
> - What opportunities will students have to help define the vision for their learning community? How will they collectively explore the question: "As a learning community, who do we want to be?"
> - How will the class monitor its progress in pursuing that vision and make adjustments as necessary?
>
> Project goals:
>
> - What goals should be universal across all of my students? What is important for all students to know, understand, or be able to do?
> - Where are these opportunities for students or groups to establish their own learning goals?
>
> Project process:
>
> - Given my knowledge of my students, my context, and my goals, what is the right level of scaffolding and support to help students navigate the project process?
> - What are the supports that I will provide to every group (e.g., project timeline, daily group check-ins)?
> - What are more intensive supports that I will provide to the groups that demonstrate the need for additional support?

frequent benchmarks and progress checks, and personally modeling some of the behaviors he hopes his students will start adopting.

For instance, after only one day into the project, one group of students is struggling to find a direction. After a mere fifteen minutes of research into traffic lights in their city, the students in this group realize that half of the traffic lights change on a predetermined schedule while others are triggered as a car approaches a red light. The members of the team aren't sure what to make of this new finding and whether or not this still qualifies as a "random event." Some of the team members suggest they move on to a different, more straightforward topic, but others want to persist and explore more. The team reaches a stalemate, with all four team members sitting at their table, silently frustrated.

As Mr. Singer approaches the group, the posture of his students seems to indicate something is wrong. "Who's the facilitator in this group?" he asks. Kate raises her hand without looking up. "Kate, where's your group at?" In a few brief sentences, Kate describes the roadblock. Mr. Singer listens intently, observing each student's expression as Kate speaks, trying to assess their reactions. As Kate finishes, he asks if anyone else has anything to add. "What do you think we should do, Mr. Singer?" Jake asks. "Well, it looks like your group picked an interesting topic—one that is a bit more complex than our coin flip!" No one seems entertained by Mr. Singer's obvious observation.

"It also looks like your group has another decision to make. Who is the process manager?" Darnell indicates that he is. "Great. Darnell, why don't you review the project timeline with your team. I'm fine with you sticking with this topic or changing it. But if you change, you'll need to make that decision today. After that, Kate, as your team's facilitator, you'll need to make sure everyone has a chance to share their thoughts about what they think the group should do. This needs to be a team decision. Pick from one of our class's decision-making protocols to help your team come to a final decision if it's helpful. I look forward to hearing what you decide." With that, Mr. Singer steps away. While he continues his lap around the classroom, his ears are still tuned into the group, eagerly awaiting to see if they gain back their momentum. He's hoping that his ninety-second intervention is the right level of support, but he's ready to circle back in five minutes for something more intensive if his first attempt doesn't do the trick.

♦ **IDEAS TO TRY**

Introduce students to a variety of different decision-making protocols.

CORE PRACTICE
SUPPORT STUDENTS TO COLLABORATE

When students engage in true collaboration, they find ways to benefit from the unique insights, perspectives, experiences, knowledge, and skills of their teammates. These unique contributions, from all team members, provide the foundation on which the team is able to co-construct novel, creative, and insightful solutions to complex problems. Therefore, collaboration isn't just a nice thing for students to do; it's a powerful tool that empowers them to tackle complex problems. That's precisely why building students' capacity to collaborate is an explicit learning goal for many teachers. (See "Getting Started with Supporting Students to Collaborate: Questions to Ask Yourself.")

Unfortunately, collaboration of this sort can be rare in most classrooms. What passes for "collaborative learning" might be more aptly described as students checking in with each other during what otherwise could be individual work. The problem students are trying to solve may not require complex thinking and may not benefit from a team approach to solving it. Even when a problem, task, or project could benefit from true student collaboration, a group of students may be ill equipped to productively work together. (See "What Does True Collaboration Look Like?")

Supporting students to collaborate requires more than determining desk arrangements and placing motivational posters on the wall. While students are the ones who actually have to do the collaborating, teachers play a significant role in setting the stage for success. Typically, setting the stage involves teachers being intentional about how they plan for collaborative efforts, how they facilitate and intervene during collaborative activities, and how they support their students to reflect and develop their collaborative skills. As most teachers know all too well, effective and high-quality collaboration doesn't "just happen."

Selecting the Collaborative Task

Lackluster collaboration in many classrooms can be explained in part by the nature of the learning task. Collaboration is a group process used to

Getting Started with Supporting Students to Collaborate:
QUESTIONS TO ASK YOURSELF

In thinking about an upcoming project (or unit), consider the following questions:

Project task:

- Is the project group-worthy? If not, what could I modify or change to ensure that the project is worthy of a collaborative effort?

Supports, resources, and routines:

- What supports will I design and employ to help ensure students work effectively with each other?

- Given the nature of the project, what student roles may be helpful? What resources might students need to effectively play those roles? (For example, a facilitator might benefit from a facilitation guide that offers a handful of facilitation sentence starters such as "Does anyone see this differently?" and "What else might we be missing?")

- How will I support teams as they reflect on their progress and develop as a team?

co-construct solutions to complex problems. If the task does not reflect a complex problem, nor benefit from individuals coming together to co-construct a solution, then it's likely not a task that engenders rich collaborative efforts.

Consider Mr. Singer's project. The project requires teams to engage in high-cognitive demand work. If a team is successfully able to draw on the resources of each team member, the team will produce a product superior to any that individuals could do on their own. Experts in collaborative learning pay close attention to these types of task features. Rachel Lotan, former director of the Stanford Teacher

♦ **IDEAS TO TRY**

Ensure that your project has the characteristics of a group-worthy task.

WHAT DOES TRUE COLLABORATION LOOK LIKE?

Examples that fall short of true collaboration	Examples of collaboration
• Having students work on a task that doesn't require (or at least benefit) from a team effort, such as a math problem that has a single correct answer and requires the use of a standard procedure • Merely arranging desks in groups and inviting students to check in with one another • Assigning a group project without establishing the necessary conditions to ensure that productive collaboration is likely to take place	• Having students work on a task that is complex and requires them to draw on each member's contributions to co-construct a solution, such as making a hypothesis regarding a natural phenomenon, and then codesigning an experiment to test their hypothesis • Supporting students to establish, monitor, and maintain a set of group processes and working agreements as they work together over a two-week period to prepare a group presentation for a panel of experts

Education Program, refers to "group-worthy tasks" as tasks that are open-ended, require complex problem solving, provide students with multiple entry points and multiple opportunities to show intellectual competence, deal with discipline-based, intellectually important content, require positive interdependence as well as individual accountability, and have clear evaluation criteria for the group product.[3] In other words, group-worthy tasks are tasks that are worthy of a group effort.

Given the student choice inherent in Mr. Singer's project, it's difficult for him to fully imagine what students will actually produce. As projects become more open-ended, they also become more unpredictable. Student products can range a great deal, along with the quality of the learning that actually took place. That's why Mr. Singer spends a great deal of time building a rubric that details clear evaluation criteria. Unlike a task that has a single "right" answer, these projects can be more difficult to evaluate because of the range of what students can produce. That's why Mr. Singer gets very specific about the learning goals for the project and describes in the project rubric what it means to master those goals. For example, while each group will explore a different topic, every group must develop and defend a viable probability model that represents their phenomenon. The model must include a description and mathematical justification for

♦ **IDEAS TO TRY**

Create a project rubric that supports students in tracking their progress toward project learning goals.

the sample space, the random events, and the probabilities associated with each event. While the project rubric helps ensure that each group's investigation is disciplinarily rich, the rubric also provides an orienting document for the team. It serves as a self-assessment and reflection tool that the team can use to ensure they are making meaningful progress toward their final product.

Setting the Stage for Equitable Participation

Even with the presence of a group-worthy task, student groups may struggle to collaborate effectively. A variety of factors will likely influence who participates and who doesn't, whose ideas are taken seriously and whose aren't, and who will carry the bulk of the intellectual work and who won't. In many classrooms, these patterns of participation can reflect broader biases within our society. Race and gender, along with other identities, frequently influence the status, influence, and participation of students within small teams. Acknowledging that these patterns of inequitable participation are likely to occur, Mr. Singer intentionally frames the work of the task to his students during his project launch. Rather than framing the task as something relatively simple and straightforward, he frames the task as complex, requiring the skills and insights from all team members. Mr. Singer is using what some collaboration experts refer to as a "multiple abilities status treatment."[4] Mr. Singer states:

> This project will require your group to draw on a variety of mathematical concepts, as well as utilize a variety of skills from your team. This project will require you to use random data sets, create probability models, construct viable mathematical arguments, and compute expected values. This project will also require you to communicate complex ideas in ways that are accessible to broad audiences, negotiate different preferences within your group, and draw on the experiences and creative insights of your team members. For

your group to be successful, you will need to find ways to draw on the knowledge and insights from every member of your group.

In framing the task in such a way, Mr. Singer attempts to publicly recognize the various abilities and skills that are required to successfully complete the project and sets the expectation that no one student can do this alone; students must rely on each other.

Beyond the nature of the task and how it's framed, Mr. Singer designed several other scaffolds and routines to support collaboration. Team members are assigned specific roles, there is a project timeline, and there is an established process for teams to check in on their progress. While teams may eventually take on the responsibility for creating these sorts of team structures for themselves, Mr. Singer's students are still relatively novice in their collaborative skills. Consequently, Mr. Singer has decided that these supports are appropriate given what he knows about his students, his context, and his goals.

> **♦ IDEAS TO TRY**
> Build a project timeline.

Facilitating Collaborative Learning

While students are carrying the intellectual load in classrooms engaged in collaborative learning, teachers are by no means passive bystanders. Rather, teachers play a critical role in observing, supporting, and intervening when necessary. Mr. Singer doesn't sit at his desk while students engage in discussion in their small groups. He walks around the room, gathering data about what students are discussing and how they are working together.

Based on his interpretations of what is happening within certain groups, Mr. Singer chooses whether or not to intervene. It's important to note that his interventions aren't designed to increase the group's reliance on Mr. Singer; they are designed to increase the group's capacity to work together. With the first group, Mr. Singer reminded students of the group roles and prompted the facilitator to lean into her responsibilities. In the second group, Mr. Singer conducted what some might call a status intervention by publicly elevating the work and contributions of a particular student.[5] To disrupt inequitable patterns of participation, teachers may need to publicly recognize the intellectual contributions of students who may be subject to low expectations or status from their peers. By doing so, teachers can help reshape students' expectations around what each student has to offer.

On day three of the project, Mr. Singer notices a troubling pattern in the participation of one of the groups exploring the state lottery. Two white boys appear to be dominating most of the group discussions and have relegated the responsibilities of Sheila, a Latinx girl, to "making the PowerPoint look pretty." While art and graphic design can be intellectually rigorous, the primary learning goals for this project center on probability and statistics. Upon noticing this pattern, Mr. Singer first decides to look at the group's daily self-reflections. To his disappointment, the group self-assessed themselves as "excellent" each day, even though Mr. Singer knew the group was not working at its full capacity. Mr. Singer knows that this particular dynamic, in this particular classroom, is actually an example of a much larger pattern in our society at large. Students hold racist and sexist biases, sometimes without even being aware of them, that influence their perceptions of intelligence, ability, and leadership capacity. It's up to Mr. Singer to notice and disrupt these patterns when they occur.

Next, Mr. Singer pays extra attention to Sheila's contributions during the team's discussions, as he does his laps around the classroom. At one point, he notices Sheila asking the group whether they had been defining their "sample space" correctly, but her question is brushed off and ignored. Mr. Singer uses this opportunity to intervene. He walks up to the group and asks, "Sheila, can you ask that question again?" After a moment of hesitation, and clearly showing a bit of discomfort with being in the spotlight, she responds, "I don't think we're defining our sample space the right way." Modeling a genuine curiosity about her question, Mr. Singer pauses, looks upward, and then says, "Hmm. Interesting—say more." After a pause to gather her thoughts, Sheila says, "Well, a sample space is supposed to cover all of the possible outcomes." She pauses. "That's right. So what are you getting at, Sheila?" Mr. Singer pushes. Sheila replies, "Well, our sample space includes the outcomes for the three ping-pong balls, but it doesn't account for the Powerball. Adding in that dimension actually dramatically increases the sample space."

As soon as Sheila finishes her statement, the students immediately turn their heads to look at Mr. Singer for validation on whether or not Sheila has a point. Mr. Singer decides to use this moment as an opportunity to elevate Sheila's intellectual contribution to the group. "Huh! Sheila, it sounds like you might have uncovered an important issue with your team's model." Turning his attention back to the entire group, he follows up with, "Everyone—make sure you are clear on this before moving forward." Now that Mr. Singer has reframed Sheila as a team member with an insight that is critical for her team to move forward, he steps away so that the team becomes dependent on Sheila's contributions and doesn't turn back to him for support. Even when students may respond with misconceptions or factually inaccurate responses, we can often find an element of brilliance in what they have to say. By demonstrating genuine curiosity for each student's contributions, we send the message to all students that each student has something to offer. While Mr. Singer hopes that this intervention will help create a new pattern of interaction and set of expectations within the group, he also plans to continue to carefully observe how the rest of the group discussion unfolds.

Supporting Students to Reflect On and Assess Their Collaborative Efforts

Inevitably, when students work together on complex and meaningful work, some things will go well, and other things won't. What's most important, then, is to reinforce the things that are working well and help groups modify the things that aren't. Mr. Singer does not leave this team reflection and revision process up to chance. Rather, he has designed a reflection protocol for teams to conduct at the end of each class session. This process prompts students to consider aspects of their collaborative work that should be maintained and identify aspects that need to change. The protocol focuses on three categories of collaboration: participation, process, and progress. Under participation, students assess the extent to which the team is utilizing the insights, perspectives, and ideas of all team members, and whether all team members are actively engaged with the work. Under process, the team reflects on their group norms, roles, and working agreements. Under progress, the team reflects on whether they are making

♦ IDEAS TO TRY

Design a group reflection
process to allow students
to reflect on and improve
their collaborative efforts.

adequate progress toward their final product. Since groups are prompted to discuss
and summarize their reflection in writing,
this process not only is valuable to the students themselves but also provides valuable data for Mr. Singer. As he reviews the
reflections from each group, he is able to see
where groups are finding success and where they are struggling. Mr. Singer
can use that data to inform the resources, supports, and interventions he
plans to provide the following day.

For example, Mr. Singer identified two groups who needed more support after reading the reflections following day 4. Therefore, he scheduled
a ten-minute group consultation with each of the two groups for the following day. As he sits down with each group, he frames the purpose of the
group consultation. "Our goal here is to build on what is working well;
we want to identify the things that your group is currently doing that is
helping you. We also want to figure out what things you want to change to
ensure your group is effective and successful." Next, he asks each student
to write down specific things that the group is doing that are helpful. After
a minute of students writing silently, he asks each person to share what
they wrote. For this exercise, Mr. Singer is acting as the scribe, capturing
the comments as students share. When a student says something vague
or unclear, he asks for further clarification. "It's great to hear that you are
listening to each other. But what does that actually look like? What are
you actually doing?" After everyone has a chance to share, he shows the
group the list of things that are helping their team and asks which ones
they want to continue to do.

Next, he asks the group members to return to individual reflection.
This time, they are asked to identify one or two challenges the group is
facing. After each student has an opportunity to share, Mr. Singer facili-
tates a quick brainstorming session to generate ideas for how the team
could address the problem. For example, a common theme that emerges is
related to staying "on task." During the discussion, the team comes to the
realization that not everyone has a clear understanding of their roles and

the project timeline. Therefore, they decide to go back to their role descriptions, clarify any responsibilities, and update their project timeline.

While this particular group consultation takes a precious ten minutes of class time, this level of intervention is reserved for only the groups that could most benefit from it. For the other groups who are able to facilitate such conversations on their own, a much shorter, less intensive check-in suffices.

♦ IDEAS TO TRY

Conduct group consultations to support students in troubleshooting the problems they are facing.

Ultimately, Mr. Singer is trying to build his students' capacity to constantly reflect on their collaborative efforts, understand what is contributing to their successes and what is contributing to their challenges, and make adjustments accordingly. Doing this requires both processes for stepping back and reflecting (through activities such as the daily reflection and these mini-consultations), as well as a tool kit of collaborative strategies (such as roles, norms, and timelines) that students can draw on to address their challenges.

CONCLUSION

Students must build their capacity to work together to take on complex work. When students develop the skills and mindsets that support effective collaboration, they are able to take on more authentic problems and develop richer understandings of sophisticated ideas. The universe of problems that students can explore expands when students find ways to work together and leverage their unique insights, perspectives, ideas, and experiences. Furthermore, the benefits of collaborative learning are not contained within the confines of the classroom. The skills and mindsets students develop to take on complex work within the classroom are the same skills and mindsets students will call upon to work with others throughout their lives. Our world is in desperate need of more people who able and willing to work together to take on thorny and tough problems. Our classrooms play a critical role in helping address that need.

Teachers who prioritize collaborative learning for their students recognize the active role they play in building a collaborative classroom culture. Far from being passive observers, teachers must be thoughtful and deliberate in their planning, facilitation, interventions, and reflections if students are to succeed.

Iterate, Iterate, Iterate!

Practices That Foster a Culture of Production, Feedback, Reflection, and Revision

Mr. Hassan's eighth-grade Spanish students are spread all over the room and spilling out into the hallway. Today there is even more action in the classroom than usual. This excitement has been generated because today is the first day of filming for a project they have been working on for the last two weeks. Next month a group of exchange students from Colombia will arrive for a two-week visit. The eighth graders have been tasked with preparing videos that will become a part of the orientation for the exchange students. Each group in Mr. Hassan's class has been assigned to introduce the exchange students to a different element of the school, like the physical space, the schedule of classes, or extracurricular activities—and the entire video must be done in Spanish!

Through this project, Mr. Hassan aims to help his students develop their command of both written and spoken Spanish, focusing on content standards related to effective oral communication, writing informative texts for specific audiences, and writing in ways that reflect the customs and cultures of Spanish-speaking communities. In preparation for filming their portions of the orientation video, the students began by creating a list of things that exchange students might need to know about their particular topic and considering the different contextual components that might be necessary to explain to help the students understand that topic. They then moved into developing scripts for the videos. In the last week, groups shared their scripts with peer groups and got feedback that they had to incorporate before getting approval from Mr. Hassan to move on to filming.

Mr. Hassan starts the class by showing an exemplar video from last year's class, requiring his students to work in groups to analyze the video using the rubric for the assignment. Each group is also tasked with identifying something that was done well in the exemplar video that they might incorporate into their own. After a few minutes of whole-group discussion about the exemplar and what the teams might bring into their own work, Mr. Hassan gives the teams a few minutes to set goals for their work during the class period and reminds them that they will check in on their progress on those goals at the end of the period. He checks the clock and gives one final reminder that they have about thirty minutes before reconvening to close the period. He repeats the mantra that he always shares before the students start their work (and that is enshrined on a *Star Wars* poster on the wall), saying "The greatest teacher, failure is!" in his best Yoda voice. "Try things out, and if they don't work, change it and try again!"

As soon as the teams start to disperse to get their filming equipment, he turns his attention to his progress check sheet for the class and is reminded of one group that is still struggling to get approval for their final script. This group went back to the drawing board a few times because they were dissatisfied with their explanations of the extracurricular opportunities at the school—struggling with the right vocabulary and idioms to describe some of these activities. The group also experienced challenges with determining how much specificity to include about the large number of opportunities that the exchange students might experience during their time at the school. Mr. Hassan appreciates the group's dedication and thoroughness, but they continue to present scripts that are significantly longer than what could fit in the three minutes allotted for their video. After their last script, he suggested through a comment in their Google

Doc that they could group the activities along common themes—for example, sports teams, those focused on games (like the Minecraft club), and service groups. He knew that this prompt would also push them to explore new vocabulary to make these groups. As he approaches the team, it is not clear whether they considered this suggestion; instead, they are arguing about how to speed through describing all of the clubs. Knowing they need to move on if they are to have a chance of completing the project on time, he interrupts their conversation and asks if they have considered his comment. "What? I didn't see that," says Allen, the group's unofficial spokesperson. Mr. Hassan asks them to review his comment and be prepared, when he returns later in the period, to share their thoughts about that suggestion.

In the hallway, Mr. Hassan finds Nadir's group already on their third take of the opening sequence of the video. Nadir is the group's director and is attempting to coach Emma through some pronunciation. "Come on, Emma! These kids are going to laugh at us if we don't get this right! You are going to make us look like fools!" Emma stomps her foot: "I am saying it correctly!" Mr. Hassan can feel the tension rising as Emma and Nadir are growing frustrated with one another—time to step in. "Let's pause for a second," Mr. Hassan says. "I agree that getting the pronunciations correct is important, but let's also recognize that this is a challenging set of phrases! Nadir, I am noticing that some of your directions for Emma are not in alignment with our class norms for giving one another feedback—keeping the feedback focused on the work and not the person. Let's reset and maybe try a different approach. Could you both look at that last take together and then practice without the video before trying again?"

With that situation somewhat diffused, Mr. Hassan ventures back into the room where he finds the group assigned to explain the flow of the school day and the bell schedule. As he walks up to the group, Wiliam calls to him, "Hey, Mr. H. I think we just realized we might have a problem. . . . We had a section of the video where we talked about the way the internships fit into the schedule, but we aren't sure if they will know what an internship is at Central School since it is different here than at other schools." Mr. Hassan remembers that one of the other groups was working on a similar challenge around context and had devised an interesting solution. "That is a challenge that is important to figure out. I know that the second group was struggling with a similar challenge. Why don't you check in with them and see if their solution gives you any ideas."

Mr. Hassan loves playing this role as the connector, and he loves seeing his students interact in these ways to learn from one another. He used to just talk with each group and give them his own thoughts about their problems, but as he has worked with project-based learning over the years, he has started to recognize that the students sometimes come up with solutions that are better and more creative than his own. Sometimes he just needs to link the students to one another and get out of the way! Suddenly, he remembers he needs to check in with the group that still has not gotten their script approved.

As Mr. Hassan heads toward that group, he walks past another group that is explaining student government and notices that the group is using incorrect conjugations. He quickly interjects: "Can y'all pause for a minute and check in with one of our conjugation experts?" He is referring to one of the various "expert" roles assigned in his classroom—peers who have strength in particular areas of the content and that other students know they can use as references during group work. Mr. Hassan developed this approach over the years both to build the culture of seeing other students as experts and also to free him to focus on more challenging issues. He smiles to himself as a member of the group sets off in search of one of the conjugation experts.

As he approaches the group, he finds them all silently bent over their laptops. That is either a very good or a very bad sign—time to find out which. "How are we doing?" "I think we've got it, Mr. H," Allen chirps. He pushes his computer in Mr. Hassan's direction. Mr. Hassan sees the silence has been a good thing; all of the group members are collaborating in a shared, cloud-based document. The group basically adopted his suggestion but with some adjustments. They are using different categories but decided to also describe one sample activity from each category—effectively combining the group's original idea with his suggestion. "I like what you have done here!" Mr. Hassan tells the group. Allen shares, "Yeah, we used what you suggested, but we still wanted to give the exchange students an example. Is that OK?" "Absolutely! I love seeing how you took my suggestion and built on it! Polish this up and share it with me, and then I think you can probably move on to filming tomorrow!"

As the class period nears its end, Mr. Hassan calls the groups back together. "Please take a few minutes and submit your group reflection for the day to me by sending an email. Let me know where you are with the project and what challenges you are still having as a group. Thanks for the good work today!"

ITERATION

Project-based teachers support their students to engage in cycles of production, feedback, reflection, and revision—a process we identify as iteration. The project-based teachers we have worked with frame this approach in contrast to what happens in traditional classrooms where students are assigned a task and perhaps get written feedback from the teacher but are rarely required to take the next step of making substantial changes to that product. Many of these teachers express concern that this is not the way things are done in the real world. Work on any sort of ambitious project— no matter if at work or in personal or civic life—requires the creation of products that will be refined and revised multiple times across the course of their development and use.

In addition, students often learn the most when they are asked to use feedback to revise their work.[1] If we want students to be prepared to engage in this sort of work after they leave school, we must structure school so that it requires substantive engagement with cycles of production, feedback, reflection, and revision. Experienced PBL teachers create projects that have explicit structures to support these processes and engage in classroom practices that support and encourage iteration throughout the project.

We begin this chapter by highlighting practices that allow teachers to track student progress and directly share feedback. Through these practices teachers set clear expectations, direct students to these expectations, develop and use tools to track student progress, and spend significant amounts of time engaging directly with the work that students produce. Second, we explore practices that support students to give and receive feedback to one another. As teachers engage in these practices, they position students as experts in their own right, actively connect students to one another, and provide guidance about how to effectively provide feedback to others. Finally, we illuminate practices that support students to reflect on their own work and incorporate the feedback they've received from peers and the teacher into new products. Through these practices, teachers build cultures of iteration that establish the iterative process as a classroom norm, create myriad opportunities for reflection and revision, provide tools and structures to support student reflection, model reflection, and help students focus their reflective energies on important content and processes. (See figure 5.1.)

CORE PRACTICE
TRACK STUDENT PROGRESS AND PROVIDE FEEDBACK

To support the process of iteration, both students and teachers must have a clear vision of where students are in their progress toward a finished project, where they need to go, and what they need to do to get there. Experienced project-based teachers build tools and structures that support their ability to communicate project expectations and learning goals to students and to track student progress to provide students with direct feedback that move students toward these goals. While many traditional teachers also engage in these practices, the work of PBL teachers tends to differ in the complexity of tracking that teachers must engage in (since students often move at their own pace in projects that extend across multiple weeks) and the greater emphasis and time commitment given to engaging with the work that students have completed in order to provide feedback. (See "Getting Started with Tracking Student Success and Providing Feedback: Questions to Ask Yourself.")

FIGURE 5.1   Iterative practices

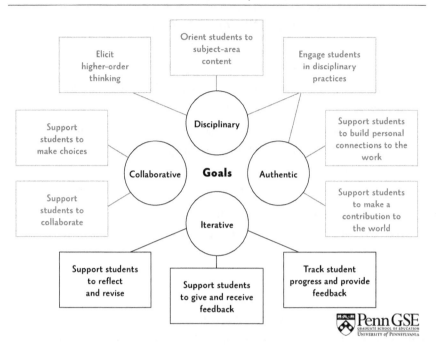

Source: Pam Grossman, Christopher Pupik Dean, Sarah Schneider Kavanagh, and Zachary Herrmann. "Preparing Teachers for Project-Based Teaching." kappanonline.org, March 25, 2019. https://kappanonline.org/preparing-teachers-project-based-teaching-grossman-pupik-dean-kavanagh-herrmann/.

Ensuring students have a clear understanding of a project and its learning goals is critical to this practice, and we find experienced PBL teachers explaining and reminding students of these expectations throughout the project. Having a well-structured rubric, detailed assignment description, and exemplar projects and using the same expectations across multiple projects are a few strategies that teachers use to make sure their students understand expectations and learning goals. Experienced PBL teachers do much more than just create these tools and share them with students; they actively use them to help students better understand the expectations

Getting Started with Tracking Student Progress and Providing Feedback:
QUESTIONS TO ASK YOURSELF

- What are the major milestones in this project?
- How can I set up student work time to ensure I can connect with each student or group at least once during the period?
- Where will feedback that I provide have the greatest impact on students' ability to effectively complete the project and attain the learning goals?
- How can I help students keep track of their own progress in the project?
- How can I ensure I have a chance to provide feedback on multiple versions of the students' project or components of their project?

of the project. We see that Mr. Hassan does this when showing his students the exemplar video and asking them to use the rubric to evaluate the exemplar. Using this rubric to evaluate the exemplar reminds the students of the expectations for their own projects and provides an opportunity to clarify that understanding. Having clear expectations for students allows teachers to refer to those expectations when providing feedback to students, an important component of effective feedback.[2]

These clear expectations also provide a foundation for tracking student progress. Given the complexity of many projects and the fact that students progress at different rates, many teachers create tracking sheets (like the one Mr. Hassan refers to in the vignette) that allow them to record notes on student and group progress on project milestones and content understanding. Teachers often use these tracking tools in conjunction with explicitly identified project checkpoints, such as Mr. Hassan's requirement that the students get final approval on their script before moving toward filming. These checkpoints ensure that students or groups receive teacher feedback on content understanding and project requirements at critical points in a project. Many PBL teachers include checkpoints as components of elaborate "project packets" that provide students with a complete guide through the entirety of the project and illustrate the depth of thought and planning required by the teacher in thinking about how to make expectations clear and identify the appropriate points to check in on student progress.

Teachers in project-based settings dedicate significant time to providing direct feedback to students in addition to the explicitly identified checkpoints. When you walk into a project-based classroom, finding the teacher might be hard because the teacher is often not at the front of the room as in a traditional classroom. Instead, in PBL classrooms, teachers are circulating and checking in with students or groups and supporting their progress on projects. One way they support this process is by providing direct and in-the-moment feedback to those students. It is not just the position of teachers that is a break from traditional classrooms, but the emphasis that PBL teachers place on providing individualized feedback on student work in process. Significant blocks of time in PBL classrooms are identified as project work time or student work time, but this obscures the fact that teachers are doing critical work during these portions of class. As teachers circulate, they assess and track student progress, identifying necessary interventions to support the students in moving forward and implementing actions based on those decisions. Dedicating this much time to the process of providing feedback supports the teachers' ability to enhance another quality of effective feedback—making sure that the feedback is given in a timely manner so that students can learn from that feedback and incorporate it into their work.[3] Too often, the feedback provided by teachers is given only after an assignment has been submitted. This feedback is important for helping students understand how they performed on a learning task, but this approach does not allow students to immediately apply that feedback to transform their work. This immediate application of feedback in classrooms is something that we know can have a profound impact on student learning.

> ♦ **IDEAS TO TRY**
>
> Build a progress tracker using a spreadsheet or table. Identify three to five project milestones to include.

A popular structure we have observed PBL teachers use during student work time is what we call a small group or individual consultation. This consultation might be one of the most frequent strategies we have observed and heard project-based teachers talk about using to support their understanding of student progress and enable them to provide feedback to groups of students or individual students. As we saw in the vignette, Mr. Hassan is not just sitting back and observing his students as they engage in the project. He is actively connecting with them, gathering information about their content understanding and progress on the project, and seeking opportunities to intervene in ways that don't give them the answer but push them to the next step. We have also seen how technology plays a very important role in facilitating these interactions. Technologies like Google Docs, which Mr. Hassan relied on in the opening vignette, allow teachers to observe students and groups as they are working on a project, provide real-time feedback in documents, and reference that feedback in conversation.

It is also important to consider how teachers deliver their feedback. While teachers might have a clear answer to a student question or know a solution to a challenge that students are facing, experienced PBL teachers often refrain from immediately providing this sort of directive feedback. As Mr. Hassan has learned, students are excellent problem solvers—when we give them the opportunity to do so. While experienced PBL teachers certainly do provide direct feedback or answer student questions directly, they often turn that question to other students in the class or group, direct the students to check in with another group who might have already dealt with this problem, or provide the students with information that moves them in the right direction without directly giving them the answer, prompting reflection. In this way, PBL teachers work to build students' capacity to ask themselves those questions and find their own answers, taking ownership over the process of iteration, and building the students' capacity to reflect on their work and identify appropriate next steps without having to rely on teachers all the time. We will deal with these strategies in the next two sections.

CORE PRACTICE
SUPPORT STUDENTS TO GIVE AND RECEIVE FEEDBACK

Think about the work that we do outside school. How much of this time involves working with others to achieve goals? A significant portion! The project-based teachers we work with recognize this teamwork as an important skill that they have to prepare students for, and they see a student's ability to give and receive feedback from others as a critical component of effective collaboration. It is also a significant source of material to support them in revising and reflecting on their own work to make improvements. For students to perform well in project-based settings, they must be able to give and receive feedback from the teacher and from one another. (See "Getting Started with Supporting Students to Give and Receive Feedback: Questions to Ask Yourself.")

How do teachers support students to give and receive feedback from one another? As with reflection and revision, a lot of this activity happens

---

Getting Started with Supporting Students to Give and Receive Feedback:
QUESTIONS TO ASK YOURSELF

- What are a few principles of good feedback that I want to teach to my students?
- How can I identify students and groups of students as "experts" in particular areas?
- When students ask me a question, do I always answer it immediately? Are there times I could refer them to other students instead?
- Where can I build in explicit opportunities for students to give and receive feedback from one another?
- Do my students trust one another? How can I build and reinforce trust between students so that they begin to look to one another as resources?

in the interstitial spaces of the classroom—the small moments in which culture is built. A central challenge for teachers who want to encourage this sort of peer interaction is the traditional vision of the classroom where the teacher is the sole possessor of knowledge and is there to impart it to the students. Teachers seeking to build a culture of peer interaction must countermand this dominant narrative and help students see the ways that they do possess expertise that can be supportive of learning in the classroom. To do this, project-based teachers redirect students to one another, invite peers to provide commentary and help answer questions, and link groups or individuals who share similar challenges and can help one another progress toward their goals. Some of these teachers have policies that require students to ask their peers before turning to ask the teacher. Seemingly small strategies like asking students to turn and talk with a partner about a concept or asking students to share ideas with one another before engaging in a large classroom discourse can build the expectation that students should see one another as resources in their learning and not

just the teacher. Small moments of encouraging interactions between students can build the trust that is necessary for students to rely on one another in more significant ways; Mr. Hassan can send one group to another because he has taken smaller actions to build this trust in the classroom throughout the year.

♦ IDEAS TO TRY

Make a classroom rule such as requiring students to ask questions of two other students before coming to ask you.

The work of positioning the students in the class as experts can happen in a variety of ways. We can see one of them in action in Mr. Hassan's classroom through the structure of the "conjugation expert" and how he sends one group to check in with another. As we also see in Mr. Hassan's classroom, small group or individual consultation serves as a significant opportunity to support peer feedback by identifying other students as experts. When the teacher connects with a group or individual and assesses the needs of that group, a common strategy that teachers employ is to suggest that the group connect with other peers in the classroom who might be able to help them. Modeling this process of encouraging

students to connect with one another supports a larger classroom culture where peers
are seen as resources that can support the
project team.

Project-based teachers also designate
groups as experts in particular areas, as Mr.

♦ **IDEAS TO TRY**

Identify some "expert" roles
that students can play
during the project.

Hassan does. A teacher might explain something to a group and then ask
them to explain it to other groups, or the teacher might identify a group
that has figured out a particularly challenging component of the project
and let the rest of the class know to connect with that group if they need
support. Some PBL teachers also identify particular students who might
be further along in a project and have the time to check in with other students. A common thread throughout these techniques is that when teachers engage students as experts, they very often do so around a very specific
skill, concept, or component of the project. Students can't be expected to
be experts in everything in the classroom, but teachers can help identify
these specific areas of expertise that allow students, and not just teachers,
to be seen as experts in the room.

Teachers also build larger structures that support peer feedback.
Checkpoints in a project are often opportunities for peers to check in with
one another. Teachers might require students to get feedback from another
group before proceeding with a particular section of their project. Experienced teachers spend significant time identifying when and how students
might interact with their peers to get feedback or to give feedback. As
noted earlier, teachers see their students as important resources and believe
the students can and should be supporting one another. Most of the PBL
teachers we have worked with hold this central mindset—that the teacher
is not the only one who possesses useful knowledge in the PBL classroom.

This getting and giving feedback cannot be done without some train-
ing. Giving good feedback is a skill that project-based teachers actively
teach to their students. They teach their students the qualities of good
feedback like those described by Grant Wiggins in his easy-to-access
article concerning feedback.[4] Teachers build rubrics about feedback and
even grade their students on how effectively they provide feedback to one

another in order to support and build the capacity of the class to support one another in their learning. Also, these teachers often model and explicitly call out or identify how they give feedback to highlight for the students how they can do it themselves.

CORE PRACTICE
SUPPORT STUDENTS TO REFLECT AND REVISE

Reflection and revision are central to the learning that happens through iteration. Many PBL teachers place significant emphasis on this process because in real-world contexts, outside of school, few products that are worth anything are built in one draft. Cars, computers, plays, social movements, books, music, pharmaceuticals, small businesses—all go through cycles of iteration that require reflection and revision. These PBL teachers focus on building cultures of reflection and revision, providing opportunities for students to engage in that process, and facilitating those opportunities. For some of these teachers, this is the central purpose of a project-based classroom: to break out of the classic school structure of one-and-done assignments and create opportunities for students to engage in projects that more closely resemble the world outside the classroom.

In many project-based classrooms, reflection and revision are in the air and the water; they are just a part of how these classrooms operate. The teachers in these classrooms spend significant time building norms and expectations that support the creation of this iterative culture. It is not just that all the assignments require reflection and revision; these teachers also continually share mantras about the importance of prototyping, design, and failure. While Mr. Hassan draws on a line spoken by Yoda in *Star Wars: The Last Jedi*, teachers also encourage productive failure and normalize the need for revision through the examples that they share and stories that they tell, explaining how they have to reflect and revise their own thinking, and explicitly identify for students when and how they are doing this. This culture is also reinforced through the expectations that teachers set around reflection and revision. Some teachers go well beyond demanding that students iterate on their written and project work by extending these expectations into classroom discourse, disrupting the traditional, teacher-centered cycle of discourse in the classroom where the teacher asks a question, a student offers an answer, and the teacher evaluates that answer. Instead, when students share their ideas, the teacher asks them to say more, challenging them to make a revision to their statement. Or, when students answer a question, the teacher might ask them to explain their reasoning. While these steps might seem small, they are actually significant disruptions in how talk happens in many classrooms and set an expectation that in *this* classroom students will be expected to reflect on statements and make changes as needed, which will be the same as is expected of their written work.

Going hand in hand with building norms around reflection and revision is providing opportunities for students to engage in this work. In PBL classrooms focused on this process, the opportunities are ubiquitous. As noted previously, many teachers start by providing opportunities for students to reflect and revise in classroom discussions, creating spaces where students can build their capacity to reflect and revise smaller ideas and statements. Opportunities for reflection and revision are also often structured into the beginning and end of each class, creating the space that students need to reflect on their work, both the process and the content. (See "Getting Started with Supporting Students to Reflect and Revise: Questions to Ask Yourself.") Mr. Hassan does this at the beginning and end of the class in the opening vignette, but what we do not see is that this is a daily activity in the classroom—a routine used to open and close each day of work in the classroom. Evaluating examples of final products from earlier students and evaluating them using rubrics provide further structured opportunities for reflection that can lead to revision. Mr. Hassan explicitly requires that the

> **♦ IDEAS TO TRY**
>
> Establish a classroom routine where students end class with a reflection on the progress they have made during the class and the next steps they must take.

groups use the example he shares to think about their own work. This technique is not just an assignment but a way of building the expectation that examples of others' work are meant to be used to consider their own work and how they might improve it. Requiring students to take this time to think about their own progress in the project—to step back and identify the next steps they need to complete and the gaps in their own knowledge—further builds culture and supports metacognitive understanding.

PBL teachers focused on iteration also build in reflection at key points in a project, asking students to reflect on progress and project forward about what must happen next to achieve their project goals. In addition to these structured and preset opportunities for reflection and revision, you will find experienced PBL teachers prompting students to reflect and revise as one of their key strategies when engaging with students one-on-one or in groups as they consult and check in on the students' or group's progress. While these teachers often give direct feedback, another tool in their arsenal is to ask the students to reflect on some aspect of their project. When Mr. Hassan identifies incorrect conjugations, he does not step in and tell the students what they are doing wrong. Instead, he points out that they are in need of support around conjugations, highlighting the need for further reflection and revision in their work. With this tool, PBL teachers can provide opportunities for reflection and revision at myriad points in a project. It is also important to consider how teachers create opportunities for reflection at the end of a project. These reflective opportunities are important not just for the students to consider what they have learned of the content (which is, of course, very important) but also to consider how they participated in the process of the project, how they contributed as members of their team, and how they grew as people through their project work.

Creating opportunities for reflection and revision within a classroom culture where such opportunities are expected plants a seed, but without careful tending, that seed will not grow. After creating opportunities to reflect and revise, experienced PBL teachers do a lot of work to facilitate this process and guide students in ways that build their capacity to reflect and revise. This effort often starts with providing students with some guidelines and tools for reflection. Students, especially those who are new to PBL, must be taught *how* to reflect and revise. To do this, experienced PBL teachers provide their students with tools to guide reflection and constantly remind them of their existence and how to use them. These teachers build detailed rubrics that are not just tools to assess work at the end of the project but also are meant to guide students in their reflection during the project. PBL teachers will refer explicitly to the rubric as a tool for student reflection and at times will guide students through how to use that rubric to evaluate their progress in a project. Mr. Hassan does this as he opens the class, asking his students to examine the exemplar video using their rubric and then consider their own progress. But he might also have used the rubric in this way with a small group during a consultation. In addition to the rubric, PBL teachers focused on this practice might start a reflective exercise with explicit guidance about how the activity will support the students' project or talk with a team about how to use the teacher's feedback to guide their next revision.

In addition to providing guidelines and tools to support reflection, experienced project-based teachers understand the importance of modeling this process for their students. They emphasize that if they ask students to engage in a process, they must believe in its importance and demonstrate that importance to their students. The project-based teachers we observed talked about changes they had made in their own project structures, highlighting how they had learned from past work with students and made adjustments. They talked about their own disciplinary work, highlighting how their work as a scientist in a lab over the summer required significant reflection and revision. They talked about their own writing process and the number of iterations they have to go through and how they took steps to reflect on what would make their writing better. Beyond modeling the process in their own work, they also model reflecting on student projects. One common technique is to "think aloud" to model how the teacher would approach reflecting on feedback that was provided by others or how to use a rubric to examine project expectations and their progress toward meeting those expectations.

Finally, PBL teachers supporting their students to reflect and revise will spend significant time focusing on the reflective activity of their students. While some progressive pedagogies encourage teachers to step back completely and allow students to find their own way through the work, this approach is not what we have observed most experienced PBL teachers doing. While they certainly do want students to identify problems and rely on themselves rather than the teacher as much as possible, these teachers employ a number of strategies that allow them to nudge students in certain directions in their reflections and revision without directly providing the solution. Asking questions is core to this practice. As experienced PBL teachers engage with groups and individuals, they ask students to explain elements of their project, prompting reflection around specific components of a project. Mr. Hassan draws a group's attention to conjugations and highlights his written feedback for another group. Both of these moves bring the reflective energies of the respective groups to a particular part of their project. Now, it is not that PBL teachers only ask questions. As noted previously, they provide direct feedback and may also simply point out an error or oversight. The difference here is that rather than correcting an error for the students, these teachers simply point out the error and encourage reflection on that component of the project.

Incorporating opportunities for reflection and revision into a classroom can be a rough road. It requires students to live with failure and struggle, not easy in the dominant school culture that rewards those who have the right answer right away. This point raises another necessary component of this practice: showing care and compassion for students as they struggle and supporting them to accept the struggle as a part of their learning process, reminding them of the contextual factors that are impacting their progress (including those outside the classroom, such as a concussion from a sporting event or the challenges of losing a friend or relative) to help them identify how to continue to engage in the powerful learning that can result through cycles of reflection and revision.

CONCLUSION

Transforming your classroom from a traditional structure and into the highly iterative space that Mr. Hassan has cultivated can seem daunting. It is important to remember that Mr. Hassan, and most of the experienced PBL teachers we have worked with, developed their practice over years of small transformations, experimentations, and reflective practice; their own classrooms are (and continue to be) iterative spaces. In project-based classrooms where students are creating a product that builds across weeks or months of instruction, the process of iteration is essential. A student project cannot achieve its full potential without an iterative process where students get feedback from the teacher and peers, reflect on that feedback, and use it to make revisions. The project-based teachers we have worked with spend significant time supporting students in this process, and we hope that this chapter will help you do the same!

— S I X —

Bringing It All Together

Practices in Action

Ms. Flores is preparing her fourth-grade students to be ambassadors at a "Kids Make History" event that their elementary school is holding in partnership with their town's historical society. The event takes place in two weeks, and it's a very big deal—especially for the fourth and fifth graders. Ms. Flores's colleagues who teach the younger K–3 grades will be bringing their students to the event as visitors. For them, this will feel like a field trip, but the fourth and fifth graders have been preparing for this event for weeks. Together with historical society staff, they have created the content for the Kids Make History exhibit, which will be a series of stations that highlight the contributions of children who played significant roles in historical events. On the day of the event, the fourth graders' job will be to guide the younger children on their journeys of discovery through the stations and to tell the stories of the children who are being highlighted in the exhibit. As they have prepared for this event, Ms. Flores's fourth graders have been learning how to conduct historical research using multiple primary sources. In addition, they've been learning about writing monologues and screenplays so that they can create multimedia exhibits.

It's two weeks before the event, and Ms. Flores's students are working in groups around the classroom to accomplish a variety of tasks. One group of four students is writing the screenplays for two videos: a welcome video and a conclusion video that will play at the entrance and exit of the exhibit. Other pairs and threesomes have been tasked with writing monologues in the voice of the historical figures highlighted in the exhibit. In a third group, students are preparing to act as docents who will guide visitors through each station. Their job is to tell an overarching story about how important children have been to major historical events. These students are busy writing their tour-guide scripts—essentially a narration that will tie one monologue to the next. Needless to say, it's a busy classroom: active, varied, and student-centered. Some students are filming videos, others are working independently trying to hammer out their monologue, and some are leafing through the sources that Ms. Flores has made available for them to research their assigned historical figures.

In this animated and vibrant classroom, Ms. Flores is faced with a daunting task: managing disciplinary rigor, the authenticity of the task, students' difficulties collaborating, and their resistance to revising and improving their first draft work. And she's managing all of these tasks *at the same time*. The simultaneity of this work is illustrated in an interaction she has with a pair of students who have been assigned to bring the historical figure of Ruby Bridges to life. From across the room, Ms. Flores can see that this pair is struggling to collaborate. Based on the progress check all students submitted the day before, she knows that this pair is writing two monologues that weave in and out of one another. One student will play Ruby Bridges as a child, and one will play her as she is today, a grown woman. They each tell different parts of Ruby Bridges's story from their own perspective.

When the pair originally presented this idea to Ms. Flores a week before, she was floored, as she often is by the brilliance of her students, but today, as she watches them work from across the room, she notices that something is amiss. One student has a pen in her hand and is busy writing while the other seems distracted, rearranging manipulatives in different combinations on the desk in front of her. Intent on prompting these two to collaborate, Ms. Flores takes a seat next to them and cheerily says, "Will you two read me what you have of your script so far? I'd love to hear it in your voices. I'll be your audience." This prompt accomplishes what she intended it to: the students have to move themselves so that they are both in front of the piece of paper, rather than having it only in the hands of one student. The students read their parts, and Ms. Flores gives them a big round of applause. As they read, she notices that, along with the collaboration difficulties, this pair is also facing another challenge: the monologue includes a major historical inaccuracy. It concludes by saying that in the end Ruby Bridges was the only Black child in her class, but she still made many friends. In actuality, after walking through angry mobs on her way into an integrated school, Ruby Bridges was the *only* student in her class for the entirety of her first year there. The story that the pair was telling was not the true story of Ruby Bridges, nor was it the true story of racism in America. Ms. Flores knows that she can't leave this misconception unaddressed. But can she support these two students to stabilize their understanding of the historical content and the nature of racism in the United States *at the same time* that she supports them to collaborate with one another *while at the same time* engaging them in a revision of what they have already produced as their first draft? This is the question at the heart of this chapter.

A CONSTELLATION OF CORE GOALS AND PRACTICES AT PLAY IN A SINGLE MOMENT

Isolating collaboration from iteration from authenticity from disciplinarity is easy when you're writing a book about teaching, but when you're actually teaching children, you don't have that luxury. Teachers don't get to do just one thing at a time, become really good at it, and then move onto the next thing. At every moment, teachers are juggling multiple goals at once: they're teaching complex historical and literary concepts *while* supporting students to collaborate with one another *while* those students are revising their work for an authentic audience. And seeing the way that these practices work together to form a sort of constellation is just as important as seeing each goal and each practice on its own.

In the preceding four chapters, we examined project-based learning at a small grain size by zooming into brief moments of teaching to illustrate particular practices. Some of the practices we've explored support student collaboration and choice; some support students to revisit, revise, and reflect on their work; some push students towards deep, disciplinary thinking; and some keep students feeling connected to their identities and to their world. We think that having the opportunity to examine practices apart from one another is important work. If we fail to explore the particularities of teaching in depth, we might never fully understand them, but there's a danger in staying narrowly focused when talking about teaching. Not one of the practices that we've examined is, on its own, transformative teaching. The longer that we stay zoomed into the particulars, the more easily we forget the larger purposes of our work. In other words, sometimes when we start to see the trees, we forget about the forest. So, in this chapter, we zoom back out to look at how the four goals of project-based learning and their associated core practices work together to make a bigger picture. We discuss how the core practices framework *as a whole* can guide your thinking as you plan a year-long course, as you plan a unit of instruction, and as you reflect on a single interaction.

When you look at any given moment of student-centered, active learning in a project-based classroom, you will see some constellation of core goals and practices. Sometimes you'll just see one. Sometimes you'll see a few in a series—one morphing into another, and then another. Sometimes you'll see a bundle of practices all occurring simultaneously. In the hands of a skilled teacher, this dance can look effortless, and practices can seem indistinguishable from one another. The important thing to know is there is no one "right way" to enact the core practices, and in any given moment there is no "right answer" to the question: "Which goal should I be focusing on right now, or which practice should I be implementing?" Rather, the core goals and practices are merely tools that can be used in myriad ways and in infinite combinations to make classrooms more active, more student-centered, and richer with meaningful learning. To illustrate how practices morph in and out of one another and often pile up on top of one another, let's return to Ms. Flores as she faces a multitude of pedagogical dilemmas all at the same time.

Upon realizing that she needs to support students to collaborate, iterate, and deepen their disciplinary understanding *all at the same time*, a question that is both daunting and familiar to anyone who has ever taught arises for Ms. Flores: *can I do it all?* Often the answer to this question is no (and that's okay!), but we want to share this excerpt from Ms. Flores's teaching because it illustrates how, when everything is working just right, the core practices of project-based learning can work together, rather than as separate entities with their own beginnings, middles, and ends.

After giving her students a big round of applause, Ms. Flores lets out a big sigh and says, "This is really going to be something special. And, man, I *wish* Ruby Bridges's story ended that way. What made you write it *this* way instead of how it really happened?"

Mariana, the girl who had been doing the writing, responds, "It just seemed too sad to tell the kindergarteners that she had to be in a class all by herself. We don't want to make them cry."

Ms. Flores turns to the student who had been playing with the manipulatives, "What do you think, Breshae?"

"I think we've gotta tell them the truth. If we don't tell them the truth, they'll get to fourth grade and feel like they've been lied to."

"That's an important point, Breshae," Ms. Flores adds. "Why don't the two of you work together on a revision—a revision that tells the real story, but that keeps your audience, the kindergarteners, in mind. You're right, Mariana; we don't want them to cry. But we do want them to know the truth. What do you imagine that adult Ruby Bridges—who's still alive today—what do you imagine that she might say to a kindergartener? For example, if she had a daughter in kindergarten, what might she say to her own daughter?"

"I bet she'd say that what happened to her when she was little wasn't fair," Mariana suggests.

Breshae adds, "Maybe she'd say that there were a lot of people who were racist, but that not everybody was and that it's important to always stand up and be against racism."

At this, Mariana gets excited, "Yeah, maybe she remembers all of the people like her mom and the therapist that wrote that book about her who were nice to her even when other people were being unfair and racist."

Ms. Flores can see that the girls are beginning to rethink their ending. She says, "It sounds like you two have some ideas about how you're going to tackle your revision: tell the truth and focus on the helpers, the people who stand up and do the right thing. There are always helpers, even in the darkest of times. Now, remember, you need to work *together* on this revision—that's what's going to make it great. This is a two-person job. When I get up and move on to the next group, what will each of you be doing?"

"I can try to rewrite it. I think it should end with grown-up Ruby," Breshae responds. "But I don't really remember exactly what happened in the real story."

"That's okay," Ms. Flores jumps in. "Mariana, why don't you help her. While she's starting the revision, why don't you reread the end of the Ruby Bridges book? Then the two of you can talk about how to rewrite that ending."

In this two-minute exchange, Ms. Flores is juggling all four of the core goals of project-based learning. She's deepening Breshae and Mariana's grasp of the *disciplinary* content, she's orienting them to their *authentic* audience, she's prompting them to *iterate* on their work, and she's supporting them to *collaborate*. She speaks only a few times in this brief exchange, but each time she's juggling more than one goal and enacting more than one practice. Using the language of the core practices, she's *orienting students to subject-area content, supporting students to make a contribution to the world, supporting students to reflect and revise, supporting students to make choices,* and *supporting students to collaborate,* and she's doing it all at once.

This snapshot into Ms. Flores's classroom illustrates how the goals and practices work together to make up the work of facilitating student-centered, active learning. For the remainder of this chapter, we zoom out from looking at how the practices work together in one small interaction to see how they work together at the level of a lesson, then at the level of a unit, and finally at the level of an entire school year.

USING THE CORE PRACTICES TO GUIDE LESSON AND UNIT PLANNING

One easy and concrete way to use the core practices to guide your teaching is to use the framework as a guide for unit and lesson planning. Whether you're drafting a unit or lesson from scratch or using a unit or lesson created by someone else, the core practices framework can guide your thinking as you prepare to use it in your own classroom. When using the core practices framework to help draft or adapt units and lessons, we like to reimagine the goals and practices as questions that you might ask of the plan. You can find these questions in appendix B at the end of this book. Some questions you ask will have to do with the disciplinary rigor. Other questions will have to do with how well you're setting up your students to collaborate or iterate on their ideas and work, and still other questions will have to do with the extent to which students' work makes a contribution to someone or something outside the classroom. While there are great units and lessons that don't have satisfactory answers to every single one of the questions about core practices in appendix B, we've found that most units and lessons can be improved when teachers wrestle with these questions and use them as springboards for revision and adaptation.

The core practice questions in appendix B can help you start the process of adapting units and lessons with disciplinarily rich, student-centered, active learning in mind, but what happens when you ask yourself the questions and then are unsatisfied with your answers? Where do you begin? Our suggestion is to tackle one thing at a time. If you're unsatisfied by your answers to the authenticity questions, one good place to start is by identifying an audience for students' work—an audience other than you, their teacher. In fact, this is exactly how Ms. Flores created her Kids Make History project. It took her years to turn the project into what it is today, but each year she dedicated herself to improving it to whatever extent she could.

TRANSFORMING UNITS WITH
AUTHENTICITY IN MIND

In its earliest instantiation, Ms. Flores hadn't even thought of Kids Make History as a project; it had been merely a report. Each student was assigned a young person to research and write a report about. Students worked independently. They found their own sources by searching for them on the internet, and their final product was a three-page report that they turned in to the teacher. Other than the fact that Ms. Flores pasted the reports on construction paper and hung them on the bulletin board so that families could see them during her school's Family Night, she was the only audience for her students' work. Unsatisfied with the project as it was, Ms. Flores started asking herself questions about the project's *authenticity*. At first,these questions were confined to the *audience* for her students' work. These questions also might support you as you think about how to design more authentic projects in your own classroom. (See "Finding an Audience for Your Students' Work: Questions to Ask Yourself.")

When Ms. Flores began asking herself these questions, she began to daydream about the possibility of expanding the audience of her students' reports. This is where the idea for the exhibit was born. Rather than being the sole person benefiting from her students' knowledge, suddenly all of the K–3 students at her school could benefit as well. Two years into doing the exhibit on her own, Ms. Flores met the man who ran her town's local historical society at a party. When he mentioned that he was looking for ways to get the community more involved in the historical society, she wondered if there was a way to create a partnership between the elementary school and the historical society. She shared with him her work on the Kids Make History exhibit, he started to get excited, and that was the beginning of a partnership that has now lasted for over five years. Like Ms. Flores, when you start asking yourself these questions, you might start to

---

Finding an Audience for Your Students' Work:
QUESTIONS TO ASK YOURSELF

- Is there a publication that might be interested in publishing something my students are writing?
- Is there a platform or broadcaster that might be interested in sharing some audio, video, or multimedia content that my students are creating?
- Is there a community organization or a business that might be interested in partnering with me for this project?
- Is there a community organization or business that might be interested in hosting a presentation of my students' work or, at the very least, displaying it?
- Can I imagine a way that other students at my school might be an audience for my student' work? What about families? What about a panel of administrators?
- Could I imagine real consumers for something that my students are creating?
- Could my students' learning be communicated to a real decision-maker or other important figure in the form of a letter?
- Can my students create something in this unit that other people might need or benefit from?

---

realize how ingrained it has been in you that you, as the teacher, are the primary audience for students' work, but flipping that script can open your world as a teacher.

TRANSFORMING UNITS FOR ITERATION IN MIND

Perhaps for you, authenticity isn't the problem. Perhaps, instead, you're realizing that your students have very few opportunities to iterate on their work over time. Maybe you're realizing that you *tell* them to revise ("make sure you're leaving yourself enough time to revise!"), but you don't *support* them to revise (perhaps by creating feedback sessions and peer-review processes). If this scenario sounds familiar, you would be in the same boat as Ms. Flores was in the early years of her Kids Make History project. In the early years, she included a series of mini-lessons on different aspects of the Kids Make History report (which only later became the Kids Make History exhibit). There was a mini-lesson on introductions and a mini-lesson on topic sentences and a mini-lesson on using and citing evidence. She was good at offering *instruction* in the early days, but her students rarely received formal *feedback* until they turned in their final draft. At that point, Ms. Flores would write on students' reports making suggestions and offering praise, but students weren't expected to do anything with her feedback because the report was already complete. This way of doing things was what Ms. Flores had always experienced in school. It was what she had experienced as a student. It was what she had seen from more experienced teachers when she had been mentored as a student teacher, and it was what her colleagues down the hall were doing. She hadn't thought to question it. But when she asked herself the following questions, the status quo started to feel a bit off. (See "Assessing Students' Opportunities to Revise and Reflect: Questions to Ask Yourself.")

After reflecting on questions like these, Ms. Flores realized that she could do many things to transform her Kids Make History project. Over the course of several years, she began instituting a series of changes—little by little—that, over time, resulted in a major transformation to the project. First, she created a series of what she called workshops. Each workshop was, in essence, a peer-review process in which students shared their in-progress work with one another and assessed each other's progress in relation to criteria that had been discussed in mini-lessons and class discussions in the preceding days. The first was the "Sources Workshop," in which students interviewed each other about the variability and reliability of the sources they had identified to research the young person they were studying. This workshop was followed by the "Idea-a-thon," where students shared and gave each other feedback on a variety of ideas they

---

Assessing Students' Opportunities to Revise and Reflect:
QUESTIONS TO ASK YOURSELF

- Where are the formal opportunities for my students to share their in-process work with others? How frequently does this sharing occur?

- What tools am I offering my students to give feedback to one another? How frequently are they using these tools?

- What routines do I have in place that prompt students to reflect on their progress toward their goals? What time and support am I giving them to subsequently take action in light of their reflections?

- What routines do I have in place that prompt students to reflect on the quality of their work? What time and support am I giving them to subsequently take action in light of their reflections?

- In my classroom, are there incentives in place (whether intentional or not) to complete work quickly and not return to it? What might incentivize my students to work slowly and deliberately over longer periods of time?

---

had brainstormed for how to tell their young person's story. Next came the "Outline Swap" and finally the "Roughing It with Rough Drafts Workshop." For each of these workshops, Ms. Flores included mini-lessons in which she explicitly taught students about giving feedback, offered students clear criteria for the feedback they would offer their classmates, had students reflect on the process of receiving feedback, and had them make plans for how they would incorporate the feedback they received into their next steps. In addition to the workshops, she added ten-minute start-of-class and end-of-class process checks in which students identified where they were in relation to their goals and what their next steps would be as they worked toward those goals. She used students' responses to these process checks as an anchor document for herself when she conferred with students and found that she had much more information about where each of her students was in the arc of the project.

When you, like Ms. Flores, start asking yourself these questions, you might start to realize how small routines and classroom processes might support you in creating a more iterative culture in your classroom. You might adapt a unit by adding in a few checkpoints along the way: one self-reflection checkpoint where students analyze their work and/or their progress using a teacher or a class-created tool, one peer-revision checkpoint where students use a teacher or class-created tool to offer each other feedback, and one teacher feedback checkpoint. Sometimes an approach as simple as this one can transform the cadence of a unit. Another simple way to bring in iteration is to add daily or weekly reflection routines in which students use teacher- or class-created tools to reflect on their progress and their work either independently or in pairs or groups. Small tweaks like these can be easy ways to begin on a path toward more student ownership and a culture of iteration.

TRANSFORMING UNITS WITH COLLABORATION IN MIND

Ms. Flores's Kids Make History project went through a similar transformation relating to collaboration. At first, when her students were just writing a report, they were each assigned a different historical figure, and they worked independently to write their own report about that person. Almost all class time was spent either whole-class (for mini-lessons) or in independent work. Her students worked in groups only when she split them up for discussions about something they were covering in a mini-lesson. By the end of the Kids Make History transformation, things looked entirely different. Her class was split into three teams: the docents team (made up of the students guiding visitors through the exhibit), the exhibits team (made up of the students creating each of the exhibit's stations and writing the monologues), and the multimedia production team (made up of the students creating the video and web-based aspects of the exhibit). Each team had a leader who acted as a project manager and who kept track of the team's timeline and progress and updated Ms. Flores daily.

Within each team were smaller teams, composed mostly of pairs, each of which was responsible for different aspects of the exhibit. While a breakdown always occurred somewhere in the system, almost all of the time the majority of teams worked together well.

This kind of transformation took a long time to make. For Ms. Flores, the transformation began when she started reflecting on how much more fulfilled and motivated her students seemed to be in the extracurricular activities she ran than they seemed to be in her classroom. She thought about how she ran the fifth-grade musical. She had one student working as the stage manager who supervised the work of the lighting team, the sound team, the props team, and the costume team (each of which had its own leader). On top of all of the backstage teams, she also had her actors who operated as their own team. And while she primarily led her team of actors, she also brought in a seventh grader to act as her assistant director, and this student routinely ran scenes with small groups of actors in the hallway when Ms. Flores was working with others. When she was running musical rehearsals, she realized that she gave her students much more autonomy than she gave them in her classroom, and interestingly enough, they seemed to work *harder*. She wondered what would happen if she transformed her classroom so that it would operate more like musical rehearsals did, with students working independently in teams toward shared goals. If she did this, she wondered, might she see students' motivation, engagement, and drive increase? Changes didn't happen overnight—and there were a lot of growing pains along the way—but once she worked out the systems that she needed to put in place to make everything run smoothly, she saw exactly what she had hoped to see: she was telling students what to do far less often, they were coming up with their own plans and solutions, and they felt so much more ownership over their work.

What Ms. Flores found through this transition is similar to what most teachers find: the success of collaborative classrooms hinges on the systems that teachers put in place to support collaboration. In her first two years of the transition, Ms. Flores struggled to find the right systems. The students that she instituted as "leaders" sometimes veered toward dictatorial-style leadership, and status issues in the classroom became heightened. She realized in these early years that her students needed as much support in learning how to collaborate as they did in learning the content, so she began working on her systems. She created a routine that she called the "team meeting," which kicked off project time every day. For seven minutes exactly (Ms. Flores was big on using a timer), students met in their team (the docents team, the exhibits team, and the multimedia production team—each of which was made up of approximately ten students). In the first three minutes of the team meeting, each pair within the team looked at the goals they had set the day before in their process check and decided together on two to four goals for the day, jotting them down on the ongoing Team Meeting Google Doc. For the next three minutes, each pair reported their goals to the rest of their team while their team leader took notes and asked the same two questions to every team: "What's the first thing each person on your team is going to tackle when we break? Is there any way that Ms. Flores or I can support you today?" Finally, each person individually completed a thirty-second survey that asked them to agree or disagree with routine prompts about how their team was functioning, like "people on my team try hard to make each other look good," and "my ideas are heard when I share them with my teammates." After these seven minutes, teams broke out into pairs and got started working toward their goals. The team leaders had a short meeting with Ms. Flores during which they reported to her about where their team as a whole was in relation to their larger goals, what each pair's goals for the day were, and what each pair needed in terms of support. Together they would go through the survey responses to see how team members were feeling about the culture of their team. Ms. Flores and her team leaders would then make a plan for how they would split up and support pairs during project time and how they would work toward improving team culture where improvements might be needed. At the end of project time, Ms. Flores always held two to three minutes of "shout-outs," during which students could publicly praise classmates for anything they did to make the team stronger, which included "going out of your way to make team members look good," "asking for help from team members," "offering help to team members," "speaking up when something doesn't seem right," and "normalizing mistakes and confusion." Years into this project's transformation, Ms. Flores was feeling great about the culture of collaboration and teamwork that she had been able to nurture in her classroom. It hadn't been an easy road, but the effort had been worthwhile.

TRANSFORMING UNITS WITH DISCIPLINARITY IN MIND

Across the years of transforming the Kids Make History project, Ms. Flores tweaked the project to be more collaborative, more iterative, and more authentic, but she also transformed the extent to which her project engaged students in activities that resembled the activity of historians and writers. In its earliest instantiation, the Kids Make History project had students learning *about* history rather than doing what historians do: visiting archives to find meaningful sources, determining the reliability of those sources, and corroborating accounts across sources to determine what really happened in the past.[1] In addition, the kind of writing she asked her students to do was in a genre found only in school: the classroom report. After transforming her unit, she got her students writing screenplays and monologues. Rather than looking at last year's student reports as mentor texts (which is what Ms. Flores did before she transformed the project), her new mentor texts for the multimedia group were a series of three- to five-minute documentaries that played in museums and for the monologue group. She also found scripts and recordings of famous monologues and had students analyze them. She asked her students to examine how playwrights established characters' voices in monologues, how they used monologues to reveal important backstory and character traits, and how they often functioned to illuminate characters' motivations. When she selected genres that existed in the real world, many more options opened up to Ms. Flores in terms of what kinds of mentor texts she could use with her students. Rather than learning how to succeed in school, she could use school to teach her students how to engage in meaningful activity in the world *outside* of school. She could see them becoming historians, archivists, documentary filmmakers, docents, museum directors, curators, and playwrights before her eyes.

USING THE FRAMEWORK AS A GUIDE IN YEARLY PLANNING

Along with using the core practices framework as a tool for unit planning, you can also use it as a tool for yearly planning. For many teachers, it's unrealistic to imagine that every unit will be highly collaborative or that every final product will make a strong contribution to a community outside the school, but by using the framework as a lens to examine an entire year of instruction, you might be able to see which of your units are in particular need of attention. To help teachers do this kind of a whole-course assessment, we created the Core Goals Course Assessment tool that can be found in appendix B.

By completing a Core Goals Course Assessment, you can get a sense of which of your units are not yet particularly well aligned with the core goals in the framework. Knowing which are not aligned can be a useful first step in determining which units to focus on as you adapt your course and work toward more student-centered, active learning. Remember, though, over the course of a year, you don't have to work on everything at the same time. Some units will be more authentic to students than to the discipline, and some will be more authentic to the discipline than to the student. Some projects will involve groupwork where students will have to collaborate a lot, whereas others will be independent with less collaboration. The core practice framework is a guide rather than a prescription. Use it to ask yourself questions and to push yourself toward the goals you have for yourself as a teacher. If it starts to feel like a checklist where you're trying to tick all of the boxes, you're probably not using it in a way that's helping you or your students grow.

CONCLUSION

As teachers, we're used to reflection. We've been doing it since the earliest stages of our careers. Each time we teach a lesson, finish a unit, or conclude a school year, we have a million ideas in our head about things we can tweak for next time based on what we learned from our students this time around. While we're exceedingly familiar with reflection and revision, one thing we often lack is a clear framework that can guide us as we transform and adapt our instruction. The core practices framework can be that guide. Use it like a north star—something to keep pointing your ship toward as you chart a course toward your destination. Use it to check your assumptions, guide your reflections, and nudge you closer to the kind of teacher you've always wanted to be.

— S E V E N —

Working Together to Improve
PBL Instruction

M s. Flores, from chapter 6, is still thinking about her two-minute
interaction with the two students working on the Ruby Bridges
story for their Kids Make History project. A quick check-in with these
students uncovered a set of demands, and Ms. Flores had to figure out how
to react. In almost an instant, Ms. Flores had to consider how to support
the two students to stabilize their understanding of the historical content
and the nature of racism in the United States, at the same time that she
supported them to collaborate with one another, while at the same time
she tried to engage them in a revision of what they had already produced
as their first draft. Her brief intervention with those students was the best
she could summon in the moment. But did she respond in the most effective way? What else could she have done?

In spite of her lingering curiosity about that moment, one thing is clear
for Ms. Flores: she has dramatically increased her capacity to respond effectively in these uncertain and complex situations. She remembers that when
she first started with project-based learning she was utterly overwhelmed
by its uncertain and unpredictable nature. The student-centered reality of
project-based learning naturally means that so much of what happens in the

classroom is based on what students say and do. Her ability to make in-the-moment decisions to respond to these moments has grown considerably.

Reflecting on her early days of project-based learning, Ms. Flores admits that most of her time and energy was spent on classroom management. With so much activity going on at once, she was simply trying to keep track of everything and ensure that students were doing what they were supposed to be doing. However, this way of responding didn't reflect her true aspirations as a teacher. She saw herself as more than just a manager. Now, she reflects on how she is able to hold multiple goals in her head at once as she listens to students and decides what move to make. Rather than focusing merely on management, she's able to push students' disciplinary knowledge, help them consider the audience of their work, support students to collaborate and make choices, and support them to reflect and revise, all within a brief interaction.

How can we understand Ms. Flores's development and growth? Unfortunately, while this sort of development isn't rare, it's also not universal. Plenty of Ms. Flores's colleagues have been implementing project-based learning for far longer than she, yet they have failed to develop their teaching practice to the same extent. Others have tried and abandoned the idea of implementing project-based learning given the complexity required to balance multiple goals and activities. And for far too long, teachers and leaders have received far too little support for their own learning.

This chapter focuses on the *adult* learning side of project-based learning. As teachers and leaders, how do you create and engage in activities and experiences that help you grow and develop?

MS. FLORES AND HER COLLEAGUES

While Ms. Flores is uncertain about her two-minute interaction, she's certain that her colleagues will have insights that will help her think through it. As she signs into her twice-a-month webinar meeting with her colleagues, she's curious to know what they'll say.

Each meeting between the three teachers (Ms. Flores and two other fourth-grade teachers at her school: Mr. Robinson and Ms. Patel) follows the same general agenda. After a few minutes of catching up, they dive into a classroom video. It's Ms. Flores's turn to present. After a brief summary of the context, she poses her question to her colleagues: "How do I support students as they grapple through sensitive subjects, such as racism, while maintaining disciplinary rigor and honoring their creative choices?" The question piques her colleagues' curiosity, and she plays the two-minute video. Given the dilemmas inherent in this particular moment of her teaching, she's glad she had her cell phone recording of the interaction. She's learned the hard way that it's easier to simply record everything and then delete 99 percent of the video than it is to describe or attempt to re-create a classroom moment for later discussion and analysis with her colleagues. Now, she records her classroom most days, which has proven invaluable to her debrief discussions with her colleagues.

Ms. Flores plays the video up until the moment when the two students finish rehearsing their monologues. Before the video clip shows her response, she hits Pause. Then she poses her first question to her colleagues: "At this moment, what are the things I should be thinking about as I formulate my reaction?" Both teachers immediately jump to the same issues Ms. Flores grappled with, including the obvious historical inaccuracy, the tension between honoring the students' first draft but also supporting them to revise, and some legitimate concerns that the fourth graders raised regarding how to address these ideas with younger students.

Mr. Robinson and Ms. Patel also surface a few additional considerations, such as a concern about a possible status issue between the two students, based on the dominance one student demonstrated as they responded to Ms. Flores's initial questions. As Ms. Patel and Mr. Robinson speak, Ms. Flores writes down the major considerations in a shared document that they can all see. After they have proposed several ideas, Ms. Flores jokes, "Great—so you can see this was a really easy moment to navigate!" They all give a knowing laugh. Ms. Patel replies, "Wait until you see my video!" While comparing each other's practice in an evaluative way is a clear breach of this trio's norms, they all read the joke as it was intended—an acknowledgment that the work of teaching is difficult!

Next, Ms. Flores asks her colleagues, "So, given the considerations we just mapped out, what are some ways to respond to these students at this moment?" Very accustomed to this question, everyone jumps in with several ideas. Some of the ideas look similar to what Ms. Flores ultimately did, but other ideas seem radically different. Without judgment or evaluation, Ms. Flores documents the ideas in the shared document until a dozen options are laid out.

Next, the trio begins to analyze the options. While some options clearly address some of the considerations, they fail to speak to others. As the discussion evolves, the three teachers begin to generate new options. Ms. Patel suggests that the teacher's response should attempt to help students consider the possible "danger" of sharing a story that isn't historically accurate. Mr. Robinson reasons that this is important not only for students' understanding of what it means to do authentic historical inquiry but also important for students to understand how inaccurate historical narratives can persist through generations and the negative ramifications that can result. Compelled by the idea, Ms. Flores asks the group to try out what such a response might actually look like. She says, "That sounds like a promising idea. Would you mind rehearsing that with us?" Ms. Patel quickly agrees, and Ms. Flores and Mr. Robinson both step into the roles of students. Given that these rehearsals of teaching are a frequent practice for this trio, they all jump right into character. The first attempt is understandably rough; Ms. Patel fumbles over her words and isn't quite sure how to make the point in an age-appropriate way. The three of them debrief the rehearsal, and then Mr. Robinson offers to give it a try.

Through this series of rehearsals, these teachers are forced to get granular and specific in their analysis of teaching. They are forced to address the question: "As teachers, how do we translate these big ideas around historical inquiry, racism, collaboration, revision, and audience into actual things we say and do in the moment?"

In the end, the three teachers share a key insight they gleaned from the discussion, as well as an implication for their own practice. Based on the insights and implications, they select a focus goal for their next meeting, determine who is up next to share a video, and close the meeting. While these forty-five-minute webinars occur only once every two weeks, the frequency is enough to sustain a reflective practice for all three of them. They will continue to consider the dilemmas they discussed, generate new ideas on how they might approach similar situations the next time they face them, and video record their classes to ensure they capture the next moment that will help them collectively dig into their practice and engage in rich analysis of their teaching.

PROFESSIONAL LEARNING
THE ONGOING PROJECT FOR TEACHERS

For many teachers, working to improve their teaching practice is a complex project in itself. Similar to how we expect students to engage in authentic, collaborative, disciplinarily rich, and iterative projects to develop their knowledge and skills, teachers must also engage in projects to improve their own teaching practice.

This book outlines an ambitious and sophisticated set of teaching practices that teachers must nurture to effectively enact project-based learning. For teachers to develop these teaching practices, they must engage in an equally ambitious and sophisticated set of adult learning experiences. Ideally, these learning experiences should mirror the same goals we have for rich, student-centered, active learning that is the focus of this book. These adult learning experiences should be authentic; they should have clear personal connections to the teachers and the work they do in service of their students. These learning experiences should be disciplinary; they should focus on what it means to design and facilitate high-quality project-based learning in different subject areas. These learning experiences also should be collaborative; educators should work together, drawing on their collective experiences, insights, challenges, and successes to help support one another and develop as a professional community. And finally, these experiences should be iterative; teachers need to engage in constant cycles of practice, feedback, reflection, and revision to develop their teaching practice in meaningful and in-depth ways.

This chapter focuses on the question of how best to work toward improving the quality of project-based teaching at multiple levels of our systems. We first imagine how teachers might come together to improve the quality of teaching in their classrooms through small teams or professional learning communities. Next, we explore what a systematic effort could look like at the department or division level. Finally, we look at schoolwide and even systemwide approaches.

In this chapter, we draw on the multiyear professional development efforts we've developed at the University of Pennsylvania to support teachers and leaders across the country, and the world, as they implement project-based learning in their classrooms, schools, and systems. We also rely on the work of our partner schools and organizations, which have built successful learning organizations for students and teachers alike, some of which we highlight in this chapter.

GENERAL PRINCIPLES OF DESIGNING YOUR ADULT LEARNING EXPERIENCES

Regardless of whether you are a teacher working with your colleague down the hall, or you're a superintendent thinking about how to transform teaching and learning in a large system, there are a few general principles to consider when designing your professional learning system.

There is a lot to be said about effective professional learning, and we do not attempt to provide an exhaustive review of what the field already knows. Rather, our goal here is to provide a complement to well-known principles for professional learning and provide a vision for professional learning that is centered on a framework of core teaching practices.

Get Clear on Your Instructional Vision

Educators must first get clear on the type of teaching and learning they are striving toward. Fundamentally, they must ask themselves: "What are our goals for student learning?" While this first step may seem self-evident, the conversation around purpose and goals is frequently left implicit and unstated. When that happens, educators have no compass to orient their efforts.

This book articulates four broad goals for project-based learning: students deserve learning experiences that are rich with disciplinary learning, authentic, collaborative, and iterative. Throughout this book, we've unpacked what all of these terms mean and what they look like. Having a shared language and understanding around goals allows educators to come together in communities of practice and work together to pursue those goals.

Identify a Core Set of Teaching Practices That Align with Your Goals

While establishing a clear set of goals for student learning is essential, it's far too easy for goals to remain a distant vision without accompanying them with a clear set of practices that help teachers pursue them. Throughout this book, we've outlined ten specific teaching practices that teachers enact to support students in reaching those goals. These practices are specific enough to allow educators to focus on a certain domain of their teaching, but broad enough to encompass a variety of instructional strategies and moves based on an individual teacher's professional judgment during planning and in the moment of teaching. Having a set of core teaching practices provides a tremendous amount of focus to professional learning efforts. The fact that these practices are tied to specific and ambitious learning goals ensures that educators never lose sight of the purpose behind the practice.

In the example of Ms. Flores and her colleagues, a shared professional vision and a set of teaching practices make it easier to have specific and sophisticated discussions about instruction while analyzing videos of each other's teaching.[1] A shared set of goals and a common understanding of classroom practices enable them to provide productive feedback to each other and to dig into the details of how to enact their shared vision.

Establish Professional Learning Goals

Teaching is complex. The list of things teachers must know and be able to do is long, if not innumerable. Therefore, teachers need to establish priorities that allow them to focus on the set of things they believe are most essential given their goals for their students. For example, if one of these goals for students is that they develop their critical thinking skills across the disciplines, then teachers may choose to focus professional learning efforts on their ability to craft strong questions and instructional strategies to elicit higher-order thinking.

Ms. Flores and her colleagues select a focus for each of their webinars based on what seems most pressing or compelling to them. Because they can't focus on everything at once, they need to prioritize the aspects of their practice that they believe need the most attention. Because it's common for us to have blind spots around our own strengths and areas in need of growth, feedback and input from colleagues can be helpful while establishing professional learning goals.

Put Teaching Practice at the Center of Professional Learning

For teachers to learn how to teach, they need opportunities to practice teaching. Again, while this advice may seem self-evident, practice is frequently absent in professional learning settings. While teachers may talk about strategies, discuss challenges, and share resources, they don't often practice the very thing that they are trying to get better at in the very spaces designed for that purpose. Imagine a theater company where actors never rehearse a scene during rehearsal or a basketball team that never runs a play during practice.

So, how can we center actual teaching practice in our professional learning opportunities? One way to do so is to think in iterative cycles. Students can learn deeply when they engage in cycles of production, feedback, reflection, and revision. The same is true for teachers.

1. *Identify a Representation of Practice*

After selecting the focus goal and practice for professional learning, teachers can explore what that practice looks like in the classroom. For example, if teachers are looking to improve their ability to elicit higher-order thinking, they could review actual videos of teachers posing questions and following up on student responses. They could review transcripts of teacher-student conversations. These examples give teachers a common episode of teaching to view, analyze, and discuss. When they have a real-life example on the table, conversations about teaching can be more complex and nuanced. Teachers can focus on the real world of a classroom, not a fabricated or artificial hypothetical situation.

Ms. Flores, Mr. Robinson, and Ms. Patel made a routine of filming their classrooms on a regular basis. These videos provided the necessary real-life examples for them to engage in rich analysis of teaching. Without Ms. Flores's two-minute video, having a surface-level conversation about general ideas would have been too easy. By grounding the discussion in a real moment, in a real classroom, where a teacher is facing a real dilemma, these teachers are forced to explore and play with the real complexity of teaching.

2. *Focus the Discussion Around Instructional Dilemmas*

Because good teaching requires in-the-moment judgment, it's helpful to focus on a specific dilemma or decision point the teacher is facing. For example, consider a video where a teacher asks a student to provide a mathematical justification for a claim in an attempt to elicit higher-order thinking. The student responds by stating a common mathematical misconception. At this moment, what should the teacher do? In the University of Pennsylvania Project-Based Learning Certificate Program, we call these moments in teaching "critical moments." These moments are critical because what the teacher decides to do could have a significant influence on what happens next. The teacher's decision is consequential to instructional goals, and therefore, this moment is worth deeper analysis and exploration.

In the Project-Based Learning Certificate Program, we have found that pausing videos at these "critical moments" and engaging teachers in discussions can produce a thoughtful and engaging analysis of teaching practice. First, we explore the question, "What dilemma is this teacher facing right now?" In the case of the student who responded with a misconception, the teacher may be facing the dilemma of honoring the student's thinking while not perpetuating a mathematical misconception. The teacher may also consider the context within which this statement was made and what the teacher knows about the student. For example, is this discussion taking place in a full class setting, a small group consultation, or a one-on-one conversation? What is the history of this student in this class? What are the classroom's norms and culture around "being right" and making mistakes?

Ms. Flores identified a critical moment in her own teaching. Clearly, this moment begs numerous questions, but there is no single "right" answer. By focusing on the particular moment in Ms. Flores's classroom, she is able to engage her colleagues in a rich discussion around goals, teaching strategies, and in-the-moment judgment.

3. *Generate and Analyze Options for How the Teacher Could Respond*
Once we have started to define the dilemma the teacher is facing, we then ask, "What options does this teacher have at this moment?" Frequently, many teachers are surprised by how many choices they can actually generate. A thirty-second teacher-student exchange that might initially be passed off as a simple back-and-forth might now be seen as a more significant fork in the road, where the teacher has a wide set of options available. For example, in the case of the math teacher and the student who voiced the common misconception, the teacher could ignore the misconception and move on. The teacher could probe the student further, asking for a clarification of thinking. The teacher could directly address the misconception and correct it. The teacher could ask other students what they think. The teacher could write the student's comments on the board so that everyone has a visual reference to what was just said. The teacher could attempt to determine what's right about the misconception and reinforce that aspect of the student's response before addressing what's wrong. Or the teacher could simply pause, raise her eyebrows, and look to the rest of the class.

Once we generate options for what the teacher could do, we begin to explore the possibilities of these different options. Rather than reducing these options to either "good" or "bad," we explore these questions: "What purposes does each option serve, and what challenges does each option raise?"

The teachers in the opening vignette committed time to simply generating multiple options for how a teacher in Ms. Flores's shoes could respond. By having multiple options on the table, Ms. Flores and her colleagues are able to assess different possible approaches with respect to the multiple considerations and instructional goals. No single option is perfect, but each individual option could likely be made better, as the teachers think through their ultimate instructional goals.

4. Rehearse Different Options
In our work with teachers at the Penn Graduate School of Education, we've found that there is a big difference between *talking about* what to do in a particular moment and actually *being able to do it*. That's why we frequently invite educators to rehearse short segments of their teaching. Sometimes, these segments may be longer, such as rehearsing the facilitation of a specific routine (for example, a number talk in a math classroom) or launching a discussion in an English language arts classroom. Other times, they may be rather short, simply allowing educators to try out the specific language they might use in the response to a student's comments.

Rehearsing these moments allows teachers to zoom into the particular and provides more nuance and texture to the professional learning discussion. This rehearsal may also surface new considerations that should go into the analysis of different options that previously weren't visible to teachers. For example, a group of teachers might all agree that the teacher in this type of scenario should follow up on the student's misconception by inviting that student to clarify his thinking. However, teachers might not realize that they have very different perspectives on how this should be done when they start rehearsing different options. Should the teacher pose a question or make a statement? How do tone, word choice, inflection, and pacing communicate different messages to students? For instance, how can the teacher follow up in a way that expresses genuine curiosity about the student's thinking instead of a gotcha moment that may lead to embarrassment? What does such a response actually sound like?

In the opening vignette, Ms. Patel's initial rehearsal allowed the trio to play with a new approach as well as surface the challenges of implementing that approach effectively. In traditional teacher professional development, it's common for teachers to *talk about* what they would do without actually trying to do it. However, when teachers are forced to actually try something, they become more aware of some of the challenges (and opportunities) that the approach offers. The rehearsals may also generate new ideas and improved ways to navigate the dilemmas they face.

5. Plan for Implementation

After exploring and analyzing a practice, teachers can consider how they want to implement the practice in their own classroom. For example, if teachers are focusing on the goal of cultivating rich disciplinary learning and on the practice of engaging students in disciplinary practices, they might determine that they want to focus on supporting students to develop and use mathematical models. Teachers can collectively design a learning activity that creates opportunities for students to develop and use mathematical models. During this planning process, they can discuss possible student responses to the task, possible solutions students may develop, misconceptions students may express, and possible areas of confusion. The teachers may also identify possible connections to other critical mathematical concepts that they hope the activity surfaces. They can begin to imagine how they might respond to these different eventualities and run through different options on what they might say and do. By rehearsing these various eventualities beforehand, teachers can be prepared to be more intentional and strategic in the moment, searching for and capitalizing on unique learning opportunities when they occur.

6. Implement

Next, teachers must implement their plans. Through the implementation process, teachers stand to learn a great deal about their students, their discipline, and the practice of teaching. How did students react to the learning experience? What were they comfortable with? Where did they struggle? Did they correctly anticipate the misconceptions that students might hold? Did their planned interventions work? What were they unprepared for? What does this all mean for their next steps as teachers? To support robust analysis and reflection, teachers can gather artifacts of their practice. These artifacts can include video recordings, student work, and their own contemporaneous notes and reflections. Collecting these artifacts helps ensure that the teachers themselves have a more objective and complete picture of what happened; these artifacts also make it easier for teachers to debrief, analyze, and reflect together.

Ms. Flores and her colleagues are constantly gathering artifacts from their practice, including video recordings of their teaching, because these artifacts play a critical role in their group analysis sessions. Before they recorded classroom video, their discussions never got deeper than a surface-level conversation about teaching problems. Actual video of a real classroom has made it possible to dive deeper into the particular challenges and opportunities they face.

7. Analyze and Reflect

After implementation, teachers can reconvene to discuss and analyze how things went. Keeping the focus instructional goal and core teaching practice at the center, teachers can review their artifacts for evidence that will help them analyze the extent to which the instructional goals were met.

Similar to reviewing representations of practice, as described previously, it's useful for teachers to focus their discussion around instructional dilemmas. Teachers can identify a moment of their teaching where they were faced with a decision, and they had to determine what next step to take. Rather than evaluating and passing judgment on the actual decision a teacher made, the purpose of focusing on dilemmas is to engage teachers in nuanced and sophisticated discussion around teaching practice. For example, a teacher may highlight a moment in a video where he uncovered that a third of the class fully understood how to develop a mathematical model, and two-thirds were completely lost. This reality—of students being at different places in their understanding and the teacher unsure of how to respond—is a common dilemma many teachers face. Now, teachers have an opportunity to explore this dilemma. Beyond the detailed analysis of this particular moment of teaching, the discussion and analysis around this moment can produce insights and generalizable principles that teachers can use in their own practice moving forward.

Toward the end of each session, Ms. Flores and her colleagues all share an insight they've gained from the conversation, as well as the implications for their future practice. While the preceding vignette describes analysis around a moment in Ms. Flores's classroom, Mr. Robinson and Ms. Patel see parallels to the challenges they face in their own classrooms.

8. *Revise Professional Learning Goals and Repeat*
The process of exploring a goal and practice, planning for teaching, implementing the plan, and then reflecting on how it went can produce new insights as well as questions. In fact, this process might surface new professional learning goals. For example, teachers might uncover through their analysis of videos and student work that they need to focus on more than just engaging students in disciplinary practices. They might discover that status issues within small groups are influencing which students have the most opportunities to actually engage in the disciplinary practices during group work time. Therefore, teachers must also focus on identifying and disrupting status issues while creating opportunities for students to engage in disciplinary practices. For the next cycle of professional learning, these teachers may identify a classroom video that features inequitable participation within small groups. By watching this video together, the teachers can engage in the process of defining the pedagogical dilemma and generating options for what the teacher in question could do to respond.

As teachers explore their practice, they inevitably learn more about what they don't know and where they must grow as educators. While this can be a humbling experience, it can also be an empowering one. The reason is that they are developing their capacity to *see more* of what is really happening within their classrooms, and they are building a toolbox of strategies and moves, along with professional judgment, that help direct them about what to do.

Ms. Flores and her colleagues have made a commitment to engage in bimonthly sessions with each other. While this is a clear commitment of their time and energy, these sessions have also served as an engine for their growth. While a given session may be particularly inspiring or compelling, it's the *ongoing and sustained* commitment to these sessions that leads to real development over time.

WORKING IN SMALL TEACHER TEAMS

In the preceding sections, we describe how to put teaching practice at the center of professional learning. While teachers can do this on their own, the preceding examples show how doing this in a community of other educators can enrich and deepen the professional learning experience. Teachers can work together in small teams using a variety of structures.

Build a Team

First, teachers can identify a small group of colleagues who are interested in exploring and developing their practice. It may be helpful to identify colleagues who teach a similar curriculum and work in a similar context, although some teachers find that an interdisciplinary and cross-context perspective can be useful. More diverse groups can help challenge underlying assumptions and bring new ideas to the table. Given the increasing familiarity and functionality of webinars and online collaboration platforms, convening teachers together no longer must fit the constraints of location and space.

Design a Routine

Next, teachers must develop a routine that works well for their team. Ms. Flores and her colleagues determined that a bimonthly forty-five-minute session with rotating responsibilities to share videos would work best for them, given their particular circumstances. Another group might determine a different structure, such as a five-minute classroom observation protocol followed by a debrief over lunch, a fully virtual and asynchronous routine where teachers share their videos and then discuss them on a discussion board, or even a more frequent routine that involves weekly co-planning followed by an analysis of classroom video and student work.

Regardless of the structure, teachers should consider how the general principles outlined here can take shape in their own professional learning experience by asking themselves the following questions:

- What is your process for selecting a focus for your professional learning?
- How are you securing teaching artifacts that will fuel meaningful discussions around teaching—classroom video, student work, lesson plans?
- How will you create norms that support the *analysis* of teaching rather than the *evaluation* of teaching?
- How will you focus the discussion around critical moments, to discuss and unpack the myriad dilemmas teachers face?
- How will you create opportunities to practice teaching in a low-stakes context?
- How will you build routines that are sustainable given your time and other commitments, while also rich and deep enough to be worthwhile?

WORKING IN DEPARTMENTS, DIVISIONS, AND SCHOOLS

Beyond engaging in professional learning work within small teams of teachers, educators within departments, divisions, and schools should also consider how to design and implement thoughtful and coherent professional learning systems. In the Project-Based Learning Certificate Program, we work with leaders as well as teachers. These leaders work with departments, schools, or even systems to transform teaching and learning. Well-designed and well-executed professional learning systems can help ensure that every teacher is on an intentional developmental trajectory and that teachers have opportunities to learn with and from one another. Unfortunately, many of our schools are designed in ways that work against these purposes, where teachers have little time and structured support to collaborate, reflect, and refine their practice. Fortunately, it doesn't have to be that way.

Develop a Common Vision and Language

A clear and explicit instructional vision—one that is understood and shared by all stakeholders—is critical to building a coherent and systemic professional learning system. Too many schools use inspiring, albeit vague, language to describe their instructional vision, leaving too much room for interpretation. When visions are not clear, it's difficult for people to know whether they've achieved their goal or not, let alone which direction they should be moving. Beyond a common image of a desired end state, an instructional vision can also provide common language that supports ongoing collaboration within a community of practice. For example, if a school determines that it values higher-order thinking, the school needs to get clear and sharp on what counts as higher-order thinking and how to know they've gotten there. What sorts of questions, tasks, projects, or challenges prompt higher-order thinking? What is the teacher's role in supporting students to engage in higher-order thinking? When an entire community has a common vision and language, they are able to discuss these questions, analyze their practice, and learn from each other.

Build Systems and Structures to Support Teacher Learning

Many schools rely on discrete workshops and seminars to achieve their professional learning goals. In many schools, professional development days, institute days, or workshop time occur infrequently at best, and often don't align with an intentionally designed professional learning trajectory. We know that drive-by professional development has a limited impact on what teachers actually do in their classroom. Rather than thinking solely about how to use the monthly two-hour in-service time, schools should consider their entire professional learning *system*. While stand-alone professional-development time may be a component of that system, other elements likely must be considered as well. School leaders should consider the following questions:

- What is the role of teacher teams in your professional learning system?
- How does your new teacher mentoring approach feed into a broader strategy for professional learning?
- How can you align your instructional coaching, teaching evaluation system, professional learning communities, and professional-development days to create a coherent, self-reinforcing professional learning system?

Note that any professional learning system that isn't tethered to a clear and ambitious instructional vision is like a boat without a rudder. School leaders need to tend to both—establish a vision for high-quality instruction and then build a system to support teachers to pursue that vision.

Consider Your Course Teams

In schools where multiple teachers teach the same course, there can be enormous benefit to investing time and space for teachers to collaborate. This collaboration can go beyond merely sharing resources and lesson plans. When teachers co-plan, implement, and then debrief and reflect in course teams, they stand to benefit from the collective reflections and insights they share with each other. However, to do so, course teams should go beyond merely sharing lesson plans and project resources and find ways to implement the principles outlined in this chapter into their collaborative routines. For example, teachers can video record the launch of the same project and analyze their different approaches and responses together.

Consider Your Vertical Teams

Teachers also stand to benefit from building a broader understanding of the learning trajectory of their students across grade levels. What sorts of learning experiences did their students encounter last year, and what sorts of experiences can they expect that their students will encounter next year? To build this understanding, many schools utilize vertical teams, consisting of teachers who teach the courses of an entire sequence. These teams can facilitate learning across teachers who engage with a given set of students throughout their experience within the school. Teachers can align themselves on what progress toward different learning goals may look like within different courses along that sequence. For example, what do collaboration and student choice look like in fourth grade, fifth grade, and sixth grade? How are teachers building students' capacity to collaborate not just within the course of a school year but across a sequence of school years? What does it look like to engage students in historical inquiry in ninth grade, tenth grade, eleventh grade, and twelfth grade? How can teachers learn from each other's practice regarding the various teaching strategies and moves that support student learning toward these overarching goals?

For any of these teams to be effective and sustainable, a school must organize its time and resources in a way that makes these collaborations possible. Unfortunately, the complexity of class schedules, teacher duties, and other constraints on teachers' time and focus can make deep, sustained, and frequent collaboration the exception, and not the rule. School leaders—and others who are responsible for establishing priorities, designing class schedules, and allocating resources—must be intentional in creating a school schedule and the necessary supports for teacher collaboration to thrive.

SPOTLIGHT
Science Leadership Academy and Inquiry Schools

Consider the approach taken by the Science Leadership Academy (SLA) schools, a set of schools in the School District of Philadelphia. Professional learning at the SLA schools is intentionally and consistently aligned with the core values driving the instructional experience at these schools: inquiry, research, collaboration, presentation, and reflection. For several years, Inquiry Schools, a nonprofit organization, has worked with the SLA schools to develop effective and meaningful professional learning that models these core values. Starting in their Summer Teaching Institute, Inquiry Schools works alongside SLA veteran teachers to craft activities and reflection opportunities that demonstrate the importance of asking good questions, providing time for exploration, sharing artifacts of learning, and reflecting on what was effective and what was not effective in the process.

As that process is unfolding, there is also time to introduce the idea of gradewide themes and essential questions. This shared focus unifies students' instructional experiences as they progress through their courses.

Teachers focus on how the overarching themes, big ideas, and essential questions can apply to their respective disciplines, looking for opportunities to make connections and craft interdisciplinary projects. Students and teachers come to understand each discipline as a lens offering a unique perspective and understanding of the essential question.

As Diana Laufenberg, the executive director of Inquiry Schools argues,

> What we want for students, we want for teachers. The best way to become better at the type of teaching and learning one espouses is to embed it in as many parts of the community as possible. A key goal is for students to start seeing learning as the goal rather than simply passing the class. Core values, grade-wide themes, and essential questions are key tools in developing this perspective.[2]

WORKING AS A NETWORK

Teachers and leaders need not be constrained by geography to work together to improve their practice. In fact, when teachers and leaders convene and collaborate across schools, they stand to benefit from the innovations, best practices, and resources that come from a diverse set of contexts and experiences.

Programs like the Project-Based Learning Certificate Program at the University of Pennsylvania convene teachers and leaders across dozens of schools across dozens of contexts to collectively explore, analyze, and develop their teaching and leadership practice. While the program hosts a multiday institute each summer, the heart of the program involves engaging in *academic year learning cycles*. Similar to the cycles of learning of Ms. Flores and her colleagues described at the beginning of this chapter, the teachers and leaders work in small teams to explore and analyze their practice through routines of planning, gathering video and student work, and collectively analyzing those artifacts. Everything we do—our planning, our implementation, and our analysis—is tethered to the project-based learning framework outlined in this book. Each cycle we engage in has a focus goal (e.g., disciplinary learning, authenticity, collaboration, or iteration) and focuses on a set of core teaching practices that support that goal.

Network of Schools

Individual teachers and leaders are not the only unit of possible collaboration. Several networks of schools share a common instructional vision and resources and supports that help teachers and leaders across the network pursue that vision.

SPOTLIGHT
EL Education

EL Education, a K-12 nonprofit organization, supports a network of 160 schools that adopt EL Education's Core Practices across five domains of school: Curriculum, Instruction, Assessment, Culture & Character, and Leadership.[3] In combination, these practices offer a pathway to propelling students toward three dimensions of achievement: mastery of knowledge and skills, quality work, and character.[4] Additionally, EL Education partners with districts and schools across the country to adopt and implement EL Education's high-quality, standards-aligned ELA curriculum and combined coaching supports to engage students and teachers in meaningful learning rooted in rich curriculum and instructional materials.[5]

To support students toward the three dimensions of achievement, EL Education devotes ample support to school and district leaders and teachers. What does this look like? At a high level, when EL Education partners with districts that are adopting its curriculum and coaching supports, school and district leaders participate in ongoing professional learning in three phases: planning, launch, and implementation, each one geared toward building shared understanding, skill building, and ongoing support for district leaders, school leaders, and teachers to successfully engage students in deeper learning experiences. Schools adopting the curriculum also receive ongoing teacher and leader professional learning around targeted areas such as assessment in daily instruction, analyzing data, or leading for equity.[6]

Additionally, EL Education's network school partners participate in regional leadership cohorts that bring together school leaders from nearby geographies in communities of practice to share and learn from each other.

Leaders might consider problems of practice and continue to develop skills to lead their teams toward greater collective efficacy. One other key aspect of this professional learning focuses on Crew, a unique element of EL Education's design that emerges from Kurt Hahn, founder of Outward Bound. Hahn states, "We are crew, not passengers, strengthened by acts of consequential service to others," and this inspires EL Education's motto, "We are Crew." Crew is both a culture and a structure that impels a school community to work together and a daily support for students to build relationships, reflect on their academic progress, and focus on character development. School leaders and teachers engage in professional learning to practice and cultivate their skills as Crew leaders to promote belonging for all students in EL Education schools.

RECOGNIZING HOW LEADERS CAN SUPPORT TEACHERS

Many teachers struggle with project-based learning. When PBL goes poorly, it can go really poorly. That makes stepping into project-based learning a particularly risky venture for many teachers. Given all that goes into a successful project-based learning experience, it's quite possible that teachers may have multiple less-than-successful experiences before they have truly successful ones. Fortunately, leaders can do a great deal in supporting their teachers.

Manage Expectations for the Professional Learning Curve

Leaders can support teachers by managing expectations about the learning curve that teachers, as well as students, may go through, particularly if project-based learning is new to them. In spite of the (sometimes long) journey to make collaborative learning happen, teachers can be encouraged to embark on that journey when they believe that project-based learning is a schoolwide focus and expectation and that they will benefit from the support from their leaders as they work to build their project-based learning teaching practice.

Start Small

Leaders can encourage teachers to start small. Students and teachers who are less familiar with project-based learning can start with shorter, more highly structured, cooperative activities that allow them to begin to build their collaborative skills. Even five-minute activities that ask small groups of students to work through an interesting question or problem together and produce a collective product can be an initial step into building the capacity necessary to take on more complex work over longer periods of time.

Consider What Might Be Getting in the Way

Leaders should consider how teachers experience supervision, observations, and evaluation at the school, and determine whether those experiences encourage or discourage teachers to work toward more project-based learning opportunities. Some teachers may feel pressure to have a class that looks orderly, predictable, and relatively quiet, particularly when they are being observed. Unfortunately, oftentimes the easiest way to achieve order, predictability, and quiet is for the teacher to assume complete control. Leaders should communicate expectations and hopes for supervision, observations, and evaluation that encourages, not discourages, teachers from trying project-based learning.

Nurture Collaboration Among Teachers

Leaders need to connect teachers in supportive peer learning communities so that they can practice and develop together. Peer observations between teachers can be a powerful tool to develop teaching practice. While this is always true, its potential power is perhaps even greater when peers are focused on project-based learning. When students are divided into small groups or are working at different things at the same time, teachers may find it difficult to get a holistic sense of what is going on, particularly teachers not accustomed to more than one voice at a given time (let alone fifteen voices!). An additional teacher in the room can help notice both successes and challenges across the various groups. The observing teacher can also gather data on the effectiveness of specific teacher interventions after the teacher has left the group (e.g., "After I attempted to facilitate that conflict resolution discussion, did the group actually get back on track?"). Peer observations can be a real investment in time and energy, so leaders must consider how to help teachers prioritize all of the competing demands on their plates.

———————————— **SPOTLIGHT** ————————————
The Workshop School

Working on authentic, real-world challenges and opportunities means taking on problems that have no one right answer and sometimes no answer at all. This work asks students to get outside of their comfort zone and confront what they don't know or understand. And it demands collaboration, often under stressful circumstances. Likewise, while we often think of centering the learning process on students' strengths and interests as empowering, it also asks them to take risks and be vulnerable. Declaring before your community what you want, care about, and are willing to struggle for takes real courage.

According to Matthew Riggan, cofounder and executive director of The Workshop School in the School District of Philadelphia, "Creating a community that is safe, supportive and bound by shared values and commitments is critical to all authentic, student-centered work. And if this is true for students, it is doubly so for staff."[7] At The Workshop School, the school's model, instructional approach, organizational design, and systems are constantly evolving. Teachers play a leading role in identifying aspects of the model that can be strengthened or improved and determining which elements of the instructional approach are most critical. Through a system of standing committees and optional design work during off-hours, staff shape the school according to need, inspiration, and feedback.

As Riggan explains, "This level of iteration and experimentation is both exciting and taxing, and often results in failure. Just as it does with students, culture and community are the keys for supporting and sustaining the work." Workshop staff have developed community agreements that lay out how they agree to work together and address challenges. These agreements guide regular team check-ins but can also be used as a protocol when difficult conversations need to happen. They are also a basis for celebration when things go well, with peer appreciations a key routine for students and staff alike.

MAKING A COMMITMENT TO ADULT LEARNING

Ms. Flores is in a constant state of learning and development thanks to her professional learning routine with Mr. Robinson and Ms. Patel. As these teachers continue to learn and develop, their students benefit. But what about the other teachers at their school? What about the other students? Are the professional learning practices that these teachers embrace idiosyncratic, or do they reflect a strategic, intentional, and coherent professional approach of the department, the school, and the system?

Schools that are committed to high-quality and equitable learning for every student cannot afford to ignore high-quality and equitable learning for every adult. We can't leave adult learning to luck. For high-quality project-based learning to thrive across a department, a school, or a system, teachers and leaders must design, implement, and maintain an adult learning system that is robust and intensive enough to meet the significant demands that project-based learning presents to educators.

— E I G H T —

Conclusion

Throughout this book, we've taken you into the classrooms of the kinds of teachers who have inspired us over the years. You observed Ms. Johnson as she supported students to create policy action plans for local nonprofits. You got to know Ms. Lopez as she transformed her classroom into one where she didn't have to sacrifice engagement to double down on disciplinary learning. You learned from Ms. Kim as she engaged her students in work directly connected to a local environmental issue, from Ms. Flores as she created opportunities for students to conduct historical research, and from Mr. Singer as he supported his students to collaboratively build mathematical models. And we also took you into Mr. Hassan's classroom—a place where every project was organized around cycles of production and revision. These educators are each an inspiration in their own right, but none of them got to be that way overnight. Their work was the result of their commitment to a long, slow, and ultimately rewarding process of transforming their classroom practice. Early on in their transformations, they committed to centering their students; to building twenty-first century skills; to seeing their students as contributors to their communities; and to driving deep, disciplinary learning through project-based learning. These commitments guided them throughout the years that they examined their practice and built authentic, iterative, collaborative, and deeply disciplinary classrooms. In the end, the changes they made did more than create better learning experiences for students; they also allowed these teachers to find great fulfillment in their work. One teacher we worked with said, "For me, incorporating project-based learning in my classroom restored the creativity and flexibility that was missing in my teaching practice. Moreover, this has been a rewarding experience for both my students and for me. I enjoy teaching now in ways that I could not in the traditional classroom. I am blooming and my students are also."

Reform efforts in education frequently overlook teachers and their daily work. Leaders argue about curricular materials, about textbook adoptions, about standards and evaluation policies, and about discipline policies—and yes, all of these things are important. But in the end, what matters the most are the interactions that students have with each other and with their teachers in classrooms day in and day out. In other words, what matters is teaching practice. That is why we've organized this book around a set of core practices for project-based learning. We believe that curricula and policies become real only through the work of teachers in the classroom. Teachers who foster collaborative communities in their classrooms can bring curricula to life, but even the most skilled of us remember a time when we struggled to get students to collaborate and iterate and dive deeply into disciplinary questions; it's complex work even when teachers have the best resources and supportive policies. If we overlook teaching practice in our efforts to transform educational experiences for young people, we overlook the most important piece in the educational reform puzzle. Teachers matter. What teachers do and don't do in classrooms matters. This book is an effort to illuminate the practices that can help realize the promise of more active and student-centered learning.

But it's not only teachers' actions that make a difference. From our years of research with teachers, we've found that teachers' mindsets make an enormous difference in the work they do with young people. As we bring this book to a close, we want to explore some of the mindsets we've identified that contribute to teachers' abilities to learn and to enact the core practices of project-based learning. We hope that they're useful to you as you embark on your own journeys of transformation or support the work of colleagues.

MINDSET 1
A BELIEF IN EXPANSIVE GOALS FOR STUDENT LEARNING

Through our years working with teachers, we noticed that many of the most inspiring teachers we worked with believed deeply that schools should prioritize a broad set of learning goals rather than just those defined in academic standards. These goals include a focus on deep disciplinary understanding and higher-order thinking but extend beyond these academic goals to include goals focused on supporting students to learn how to interact with one another; how to prototype, fail, and develop new ideas; and how to engage with the world beyond classroom walls. We believe that this broader set of goals is absolutely necessary to prepare students for all that they will face in the world beyond school. For example, Mr. Singer's focus on building students' capacity to work together prepares them to work with others in ways that will be critical to the success in their careers and lives as citizens.

The complex problems that the world faces cannot be addressed by individuals alone, and project-based learning helps students learn how to tackle challenges as a group. Traditional schooling's focus on individual performance and competition can actually inhibit the development of these important skills for working with others. Clearly, this is not a new idea. Educational philosophers, like John Dewey, have been making this point for over a century, yet all too often classrooms prioritize the work of individuals over the work of a team, individual success over collective accomplishment. Preparing students to work together is not just a nice additional skill for students to learn; it is an essential component of preparing students for the world.

The focus on iteration in project-based classrooms is another example of this expanded set of learning goals that project-based learning enables. Too often, the rush to cover a broad range of academic material does not allow students to develop the ability to use feedback to revise their work; instead, students have to submit their test or paper and then move immediately on to the next topic. Project-based learning provides teachers with the opportunity to engage students with iterative processes and helps them understand the value of feedback and the necessity of revision for quality work. Our first attempts at new projects are not typically our best attempts, but if we are never offered opportunities to revise and adapt, we will never know what we are capable of. Bringing project-based learning into the classroom allows teachers to support students around this critical learning goal.

While the most inspiring teachers with whom we have worked have emphasized the necessity of focusing on these additional learning goals, they have also identified the need to examine the subject area learning goals that are often the main driver of the curriculum. Unfortunately, some educational policies and testing requirements push teachers and administrators to prioritize coverage of content knowledge rather than the development of deep understanding. While these policies are changing in some places, too often this approach leads to a belief that the broader set of learning goals we've identified, and the sort of deep disciplinary learning sought by many project-based learning teachers, is impossible to achieve because of a need to address content standards. And given the emphasis on high-stakes testing and accountability over the past decade, we can see how easy it would be to give up on these expanded goals. However, some of the most inspiring teachers that we've gotten to know believe strongly that focusing on broader skills and capabilities actually enhances students' capacity and motivation to learn necessary content. In fact, some of the most recent research on the implementation of project-based learning in Advanced Placement classrooms indicates that students engaged in high-quality project-based learning versions of these courses outperform their peers in traditional classrooms on the same AP tests.[1]

Other teachers we've worked with argue that content standards are actually insufficient markers of disciplinary learning. They claim that project-based learning allows students to learn the work of the discipline more authentically—by playing the game rather than watching from the sidelines—by doing science, history, or mathematics rather than just learning facts about those disciplines. While basic content knowledge provides students with the knowledge and skills they may need to engage in higher-order thinking and disciplinary work, we share the belief of many teachers that through project-based learning, teachers can create opportunities for students to engage in this high-level disciplinary work while also building necessary basic knowledge and skills. We believe, however, that being able to do so requires teachers to focus on their capacity to enact many of the practices that we have described in this book.

MINDSET 2
A BELIEF THAT STUDENTS ARE CAPABLE

The second mindset shared by the most inspiring teachers with whom we've worked is a deep belief that students are capable—and not just capable of doing well on tests, but capable of making meaningful contributions to the world. Teachers who embrace project-based learning believe that their students are capable of supporting one another, of leading their own learning, of meaningfully contributing to their schools and communities, not just in the future, but right now. We have seen this deep belief in students as a major driver for teachers who are actively working to decenter themselves in the classroom and center the students as leaders of their own learning. They believe their students are capable of much more than what they are often asked to do in school and deserve more than acting as passive recipients of lessons being delivered by the teacher.

Let's start with the teachers' belief in the ability of students to support one another. In many of the vignettes in this book, we see students supporting one another through activities and projects. Sometimes this support is informal, in the ways that groups are working together to solve problems, such as when Mr. Hassan leaves a group to figure out how to restructure their video after providing a little direction, or more formal like when Mr. Hassan sends a team to the "conjugation experts" to revise their script. This approach is not just a strategy to reduce the number of

questions the teacher has to answer in a class period, although it does help
with that! Instead, directing students to learn from one another reflects
the belief that this approach can support student learning of both content
and the broader skills of collaboration. There is an often-used phrase in
education: "The one who does the work does the learning." When teachers
do all the intellectual work of posing and answering questions, students
have fewer opportunities to internalize the intellectual skills and content.
When teachers direct students to support one another, the students are
doing the intellectual work. Teachers who do not see their students as
capable of supporting one another in these ways limit their ability to learn
from these experiences. Project-based learning is structured to create more
of these opportunities for students to rely on and learn from one another.
Teachers therefore must trust the students and believe in their capabilities to do this work, but PBL also requires that teachers engage in specific practices that create opportunities for these engagements and support
students to learn the skills and attitudes necessary to effectively support
one another.

Another way this mindset has an impact on teacher practice is that
teachers who believe their students are capable are more likely to let their
students take charge of their own learning. To do so, they create opportunities for students to make meaningful choices about what and how they
will learn. In some schools where all or most of the teachers use project-
based learning, this encouragement of student choice and agency builds
across the grades to the point where students create and conduct projects
entirely of their own design. This approach makes sense for teachers who
are seeking to prepare students to make choices in their postsecondary
lives, careers, and civic engagement. While creating opportunities for student choice might be a good way to prepare students for their civic and
professional lives, it's also a part of *disciplinary* learning. Supporting students to determine how to approach disciplinary problems, rather than
providing them with strict, preset procedures about how to approach
those problems, is more in line with how disciplinary scholars do their
work. Mathematicians, scientists, and historians are constantly making
decisions about which problems to focus on and how to pursue rigorous

answers or solutions. Of course, encouraging students to tackle problems on their own does not mean that teachers shouldn't help students learn how to approach and make decisions about approaching problems—scaffolding is key—but all too often schools do little to move students toward growing agency around their work. Highly skilled project-based learning practitioners use projects to create opportunities for student choice and engage in practices that support students to learn how to approach these choices.

Finally, this belief in the capabilities of students manifests in the way that teachers view their students' capacity to make contributions to the communities around them. School is often seen solely as preparation for the future. Teachers using project-based learning have the opportunity to see schools and their students differently. Through authentic projects, students can be positioned as capable of making contributions right now. Teachers see students not as potential participants in society in a distant future but as valuable actors in the current moment. This change can have a significant impact on the way both teachers and students approach their work. If students are making a presentation to a local nonprofit board, sending a letter to an editor, or producing a video for their school, their work has a real impact on others; it is not just a grade in a teacher's gradebook. This shift cannot happen unless teachers have a deep and fundamental belief that their students are capable of making these contributions to their broader community and the skills necessary to support students to be successful.

MINDSET 3
A COMMITMENT TO EQUITY AND LIBERATION

Along with thinking beyond academic standards and believing strongly that their students are capable, the most inspiring project-based learning teachers we have known have been those who center equity in their work. They know that access to student-centered learning has never been an equitably distributed resource in our society. Teachers who do this work well understand that they are working against long legacies of racism and classism in education. These legacies have meant that policies and curricula promoting rote and decontextualized instruction are disproportionately found in schools serving students of color and students impacted by poverty. In contrast, across town in white and affluent communities, educational leaders are more likely to push for student voice and choice and authentic projects. This trend of stark differences in the type of education provided to students from different backgrounds is nothing new. In 1980, the researcher Jean Anyon published a study that examined the types of work students from different social classes were asked to do in school.[2] In this essay she argued that there was a "hidden curriculum" that perpetuated societal inequalities through the type of work assigned in schools attended by students from different social classes. What she found in the five schools that she profiled was that students in "working" and "middle class" schools were expected to do work that was largely rote and learned that following directions and getting the right answer were the paths to academic success. The instruction in those schools looked largely like the type of instruction and classroom environment that the project-based learning practitioners we have worked with over the years are working to change. Students in the schools Anyon identified as "affluent" and "elite" were more likely to be asked to do work that cultivated conceptual understanding, creativity, and analytic skills that are more similar to the goals of high-quality project-based learning curriculum and effective project-based learning practitioners.

As Anyon's study showed back in the 1980s (along with many, many others in the decades since), the history of student-centered pedagogy is not an apolitical one. This is something that the most skilled project-based teachers understand deeply. Through our work, we've gotten to meet many of these teachers and learn about how, in order to bring project-based learning into poverty-impacted schools, they have had to fight against pervasive racist and classist beliefs, embedded in existing policies, curricula, and practices. These teachers understand that they are fighting against legacies of oppression when they position their students as young people with agency who can be trusted to lead their own learning. They understand that when they center their students' voices, interests, and knowledge, they are engaging in a countercultural practice—one that sees students and their communities as producers of knowledge rather than as consumers of knowledge produced by others long ago. They understand that traditional pedagogical approaches center the perspectives of the dominant culture and that by centering their students, they are turning the tables, not only on traditional pedagogy, but on long legacies of oppression that have negatively affected the communities they serve.

Of course, this does not mean that all the teachers with whom we have worked have jettisoned their curricula. Rather, they have found ways to bring in student voices and to open dialogues about the relevance of the curriculum to the lives of the students in the classroom. In doing so, project-based learning teachers have broadened the questions to be considered in school, enabling the emergence of culturally relevant pedagogy that is grounded in the lives of the students in that classroom and not based on assumptions about what is culturally relevant to those students. This is one way that project-based learning teachers focus on equity: by centering student voice, choice, agency, and contributions to their communities. As with the other mindsets, bringing this to fruition is not easy and requires that teachers refine their practice in ways that support and engage the voice of students.

This disparity in access to student-centered pedagogy highlights both the potential of and a critical challenge for project-based learning. When high-quality project-based learning is effectively implemented in poverty-impacted schools, it can have a transformational impact, teaching young people that their voices, their ideas, and their communities matter. This is what our students deserve. However, what we often see is that project-based learning is more frequently adopted in schools like the affluent and elite schools that Anyon described. If this trend continues, it will simply perpetuate the structural differences that Anyon identified forty years ago. In other words, project-based learning has significant potential to transform schools and address social inequity but *only if access and implementation of this practice are distributed equitably*. This focus on bringing project-based learning to students who all too often don't have the opportunity to experience it is a driving motivator of many teachers we have worked with; they provide a vision of what is possible. We hope that this book provides another tool for those who are seeking to transform their classrooms and the experiences their students have to ensure that project-based learning is a pedagogy that is accessible by all students rather than those who are already advantaged.

MINDSET 4
A BELIEF THAT TEACHERS ARE ALWAYS LEARNING

I love being a teacher. To me, being a teacher does not mean being a missionary, or having received a certain command from heaven. Rather, a teacher is a professional, one who must constantly seek to improve and to develop certain qualities or virtues, which are not received but must be created.

—*Paulo Freire*[3]

Like Paulo Freire, the teachers we have had the privilege to work with love teaching, and they believe that they have a responsibility to continually improve their practice as educators. Many feel a similar responsibility to continue to explore and learn about their content area and contribute to their communities. They see project-based learning as a powerful tool for doing so. As they encourage students to engage in iteration, they actively model this iteration in their own practice, talking about the changes they have made in the projects across the years. As they engage in disciplinary problems with their students, they demonstrate their eagerness as learners of the subject matter they teach by illustrating how they are continuing to learn and explore the content. They engage with their students in the problems posed in the projects they assign because they find them authentically engaging. Teachers love project-based learning in part because it allows them to engage as learners alongside their students.

Freire describes "humility" as one of the qualities that teachers must continually seek to develop: "Humility accepts the need we have to learn and relearn again and again, the humility to know with those whom we help to know."[4] Where some teachers feel the need to position themselves as the ultimate authority on their subject, teachers who embrace project-based learning tend to be humble, to position themselves as learners alongside their students. In fact, this is what some teachers say keeps them excited about project-based learning. They have the opportunity to engage in novel investigations with each new set of students, in the process of continuing to learn and develop their own knowledge and skills both as a teacher and as a student of the subject they teach.

Teaching is hard work. There is always more for us to learn as professionals and as individuals—always ways we can learn to better support the students we work with. But the knowledge that students rely on us, that we have a formative impact on the students we work with, weighs heavily on the minds of most teachers. There is an urgency implicit in the work of teaching because we know that students and parents are depending on us, relying on us to do our job well. This is even more true in communities where educational institutions have to struggle against their own histories of underserving their communities due to legacies of racism and classism. These realities lead many teachers to work late into the night, fret over their students, and criticize themselves when they fail. As educators, we feel the immense urgency to support the students we work with. But we also have to recognize that we are each human—limited in how much and how quickly we can learn and grow as professionals in our practice.

Turning to Freire again can help us consider this tension—between our urgent need to do right by our students *at this very moment* and our knowledge that our own professional learning will take time. Of this tension, Freire said,

> Another important virtue for the teacher is patience and its opposite, impatience. We teachers must learn how to make a life together with our students who may be different from us. This kind of learning implies patience and impatience. We must always be impatient about achieving our dream and helping students achieve theirs. Yet if we and our students push too hard and too fast for our dreams, we may destroy them. Thus, we must be patiently impatient.[5]

For those embarking on the journey of becoming project-based learning educators, this quote speaks to the challenges of transforming classroom practice. We must balance the responsibility to care for and support the learning of students in our classroom right now with the fact that we have so much to learn ourselves, as we continue to grow as educators. We must do it all now, for the sake of our students, and we cannot do it all now, because learning takes time—a paradox at the center of being a teacher. There is comfort, at least, in knowing that we are not alone in confronting this dilemma. There is a vast community of educators out there wrestling through this same contradiction, striving to do right by their students every day, sometimes falling short but always moving forward. Reaching out to members of this community for support, advice, and encouragement is a critical part of the journey toward transforming practice.

The process of writing this book has allowed us opportunities to consider the inspiring work of the teachers we have had the privilege of working with over many years and has kept us connected to the power, the intricacy, and the consistent imperfection of teaching. And it has reminded us of exactly how much teaching matters. Classrooms are microcosms of society, and what happens within their four walls has enormous consequences—not just for the students in any given school year, but for the civic communities and world they will help build in the future.

Amidst the hustle and bustle of the daily work in schools, it's sometimes hard to remember that what teachers are doing is growing a generation—one that will, like every generation before it, change the world. And just as cliffs are shaped by the crashing of waves over time—it's the small things that teachers repeat over and over again that will do the shaping—the way teachers ask students for their ideas, the way they support their students to work with others, the way teachers push students to prototype and iterate and to make contributions to their communities—those small, consistent, routine practices will slowly, but undoubtedly, shape them. While this can feel like a daunting responsibility, it is also the gift of our profession—to be the consistent and nurturing wave that shapes the next generation, little by little, every day.

Resources for Project-Based Learning

LER RESOURCES
https://sprocket.lucasedresearch.org/

The Lucas Education Research (LER) Foundation has funded numerous research projects that investigate project-based curricula. Out of these research projects, LER has created Sprocket, an online portal where teachers can access full-year project-based curricula. It also includes an online community where teachers are able to share ways to implement and adapt the courses. Currently, access to Sprocket is by invitation only, but interested teachers can contact LER at admin@lucasedresearch.org to inquire about gaining access.

PBLWORKS
https://www.pblworks.org

PBLWorks is a professional development provider, designer of educational resources, and research organization that is exclusively focused on project-based learning. The organization has an explicit focus on equity and access in project-based learning, stating "Our exclusive focus is Project Based Learning. Why? Because PBL advances educational equity and empowers youth furthest from opportunity. We believe PBL is transformative for all kids. Through PBL, students engage in learning that is deep, long-lasting, and relevant to the challenges of their lives and the world they will inherit." PBLWorks offers workshops and support services around project-based learning for teachers, schools, district leaders, and instructional coaches. Additionally, the organization provides tools for planning and implementing project-based learning and conduct research on its efficacy.

EL EDUCATION
https://eleducation.org/

EL Education, a K–12 nonprofit organization, supports a network of 160 schools that adopt EL Education's Core Practices across five domains of school: Curriculum, Instruction, Assessment, Culture & Character, and Leadership. In combination, these practices offer a pathway to propelling students toward three dimensions of achievement: mastery of knowledge and skills, quality work, and character. Additionally, EL Education partners with districts and schools across the country to adopt and implement EL Education's high-quality, standards-aligned ELA curriculum and combined coaching supports to engage students and teachers in meaningful learning rooted in rich curriculum and instructional materials.

HIGH TECH HIGH
https://www.hightechhigh.org

High Tech High began in 2000 as a small public charter school in San Diego and has now grown into a network of sixteen schools and a High Tech High Graduate School of Education offering professional development around project-based learning, including PBL design camps and a leadership academy. The organization's guiding principles echo the emphasis on collaboration, personalization, equity, and authenticity that threads throughout our book. Its website includes a curated set of student projects to provide teachers with ideas and access to *UnBoxed*, a Journal for Adult

Learning in Schools, which includes numerous resources for educators, including PBL Essentials for teachers who want to learn more about PBL.

EDUTOPIA
https://www.edutopia.org

Edutopia is a widely respected website focused on using stories of innovation and continuous learning to show people how to adopt or adapt best practices in education. Its vision "is of a new world of learning based on the compelling truth that improving education is the key to the survival of the human race. It's a world of creativity, inspiration, and ambition informed by evidence and experience." The site contains articles and videos on a wide range of topics in K–12 education. The site is a part of the George Lucas Educational Foundation.

TRANSCEND
www.transcendeducation.org

Transcend is a nonprofit organization that is guided by five fundamental beliefs: (1) All children have infinite potential; (2) to realize this potential, we must reimagine "schooling" as we know it; (3) the work is most successful when pursued through a rigorous, community-driven R&D process grounded in equity; (4) while never easy, innovation is absolutely possible, and (5) accelerating progress requires strong local leadership, surrounded by a conducive ecosystem. Transcend offers free resources to teachers, leaders, and other educators on its website.

Tools for Teachers

CORE PRACTICE PLANNING REFLECTION QUESTIONS

Core goals	Core practice	Questions to ask of your unit or lesson
Disciplinary	Elicit higher-order thinking	• What questions, prompts, or problems are presented to students? • To what extent will these questions, prompts, or problems require students to synthesize, evaluate, justify, or defend ideas? • How frequently are students engaging with these types of questions, prompts, or problems? • Would it be possible to engage in this unit or lesson without synthesizing, evaluating, justifying, or defending ideas? • Am I engaging students in tasks that are inherently open-ended or uncertain? How frequently?
	Orient students to subject area content	• What core disciplinary ideas and/or skills am I working on? Are these core ideas and skills meaningful and important in the discipline or subject area? Why? • Look at the work that students are asked to do (not at the explanations that teachers are giving). To what extent is students' work tightly connected to core ideas and skills of the subject area? • Would it be possible for students to complete their work without deeply understanding these core ideas or skills?

Core goals	Core practice	Questions to ask of your unit or lesson
Disciplinary, *continued*	Engage Students in Disciplinary Practices	• Where are students doing things that experts in this discipline or field do (e.g., designing experiments like a scientist, corroborating evidence across artifacts or primary source documents like a historian, determining the constitutionality of a law like a judge)? • Are students more frequently engaged in tasks like those in the preceding question, or are they more frequently engaged in tasks that only students do (e.g., taking notes on a lecture, studying for a test, answering multiple-choice questions)?
Authenticity	Support students to build personal connections to their work	• Where are students explicitly asked to consider how their personal stances, beliefs, experiences, values, or views relate to their project? How frequently does this occur? • Where are students asked to share their unique knowledge (things they know or believe because of their family, community, culture, or interests) rather than things they know because of this class or classes like it? How frequently does this occur?
	Support students to make a contribution to the world	• Who will see students' work? Is it only the teacher or the teacher and other students in the class? If so, what other audiences might be created? • Are the students creating something that makes a concrete contribution to someone or something outside of the classroom? • Where are students using materials that have meaning outside of the classroom? (*Examples of materials that don't have meaning outside of the classroom include textbooks, tests, and handouts. Examples of materials that do have meaning outside of the classroom include novels, lab equipment, primary source documents, and datasets.*)
Collaborative	Support students to make choices	• Where am I giving students opportunities to make real and consequential choices? • What support am I providing so that all students develop as thoughtful decision-makers?

Core goals	Core practice	Questions to ask of your unit or lesson
Collaborative, *continued*	Support students to collaborate	• What tasks, if any, are students asked to do for which interdependence is required and for which working in a group would actually improve the quality of the end product? If none or few, how can I change the tasks to make them group worthy?
		• What opportunities am I providing for students to work together on meaningful and interdependent work?
		• How am I monitoring student participation within groups, and what supports am I providing to encourage equitable participation?
		• What am I doing to preempt status issues within groups? What plans do I have to disrupt harmful or unproductive patterns of talk and participation in groups?
Iterative	Support students to reflect and revise	• What intentional opportunities am I creating for students to reflect on their work? How frequently am I asking them to reflect on their work and on their progress?
		• How am I supporting students to use their reflections to revise and improve their work?
	Support students to give and receive feedback	• What intentional opportunities am I giving students to review each other's work and provide feedback?
		• What supports do students need to give and receive high-quality feedback? How are they getting these supports?
	Track student progress and provide feedback	• Are students producing a final product? What is it? What steps are they taking to get there? How many stages does the product go through before it is complete?
		• How am I assessing or tracking the progress of each student through these stages? What data am I gathering about where each student is? How frequently do I gather this data and how?
		• Where are these opportunities for me to use that data I'm collecting to support each student? What are they getting from me at each stage? How will what they get from me support them moving forward?
		• Where do I support students to engage in self-assessment or self-tracking? What tools are students using for this?

CORE GOALS COURSE ASSESSMENT TOOL

	Disciplinary	Authentic	Iterative	Collaborative
	Students grapple with big ideas that are central in the discipline by doing things that people in the discipline do.	Students' work has an authentic audience and makes a real contribution to the world.	Students are supported to continually reflect, revise, and prototype a final product.	Students have significant opportunity to engage in interdependent tasks with others.
	A lot/A little/ Not much	A lot/A little/ Not much	A lot/A little/ Not much	A lot/A little/ Not much
Project 1				
Project 2				
Project 3				
Project 4				
Project 5				
Project 6				

NOTES

CHAPTER 1

1. "5 Keys to Rigorous Project-Based Learning," Edutopia, June 25, 2014, https://www
.edutopia.org/; John Larmer, John R. Mergendoller, and Suzie Boss, *Setting the Standard for Project Based Learning: A Proven Approach to Rigorous Classroom Instruction* (Alexandria, VA: ASCD, 2015); John W. Thomas, "A Review of Research on Project-Based Learning," Bob Pearlman, March 2000, http://www.bobpearlman.org/BestPractices/PBL_Research.pdf.

2. Brendan Moss, "Governor Baker Signs Bill to Promote Civic Education for Students," Mass.gov, November 8, 2018, https://www.mass.gov/news/governor-baker-signs-bill-to-promote-civic-education-for-students.

3. Pamela L. Grossman, *Teaching Core Practices in Teacher Education* (Cambridge, MA: Harvard Education Press, 2018).

4. "Great Teachers Aren't Born. They're Taught," TeachingWorks, 2020, http://www.teaching works.org/.

5. Bradley Fogo, "Core Practices for Teaching History: The Results of a Delphi Panel Survey," *Theory & Research in Social Education* 42, no. 2 (2014): 151–96, https://doi.org/10.1080/0093 3104.2014.902781; Matthew Kloser, "Identifying a Core Set of Science Teaching Practices: A Delphi Expert Panel Approach," *Journal of Research in Science Teaching* 51, no. 9 (November 1, 2014): 1185–1217, https://doi.org/10.1002/tea.21171.

6. "Knowledge in Action Research: Helping to Make the Case for Rigorous Project-Based Learning," Edutopia, October 17, 2013, https://www.edutopia.org/package/knowledge-action-research-helping-make-case-rigorous-project-based-learning.

CHAPTER 2

1. Suzanne H. Chapin, Catherine O'Conner, and Nancy Canavan Anderson, *Talk Moves: A Teacher's Guide for Using Classroom Discussions in Math, Grades K–6*, 3rd ed. (Sausalito, CA: Math Solutions, 2013).

2. Mark Windschitl, Jessica Thompson, and Melissa Braaten, *Ambitious Science Teaching* (Cambridge, MA: Harvard Education Publishing Group, 2018).

3. James W. Stigler and James Hiebert, *The Teaching Gap: Best Ideas from the World's Teachers for Improving Education in the Classroom* (New York, NY: Free Press, 2009).

4. Create for STEM Institute, "Multiple Literacies in Project-Based Learning (PBL)," Michigan State University, 2015, https://create4stem.msu.edu/projects/projects_listing/multiple_literacies_project_based_learning_pbl.

5. Samuel S. Wineburg and Pamela L. Grossman, *Interdisciplinary Curriculum: Challenges to Implementation* (New York, NY: Teachers College Press, 2000).

6. Lee Shulman, "Knowledge and Teaching: Foundations of the New Reform," *Harvard Educational Review* 57, no. 1 (1987): 1–23.

7. Peter B. Dow, "Man: A Course of Studying Retrospect: A Primer for Curriculum in the 70's," *Theory into Practice* 10, no. 3 (1971): 168–77; Gerald Holton, "Harvard Project Physics: A Report on Its Aims and Current Status," *Physics Education* 4, no. 1 (1969): 19–25.

8. Jerome S. Bruner, *The Process of Education* (Cambridge, MA: Harvard University Press, 1977).

CHAPTER 3

1. Gloria Ladson-Billings, "But That's Just Good Teaching! The Case for Culturally Relevant Pedagogy," *Theory into Practice* 34, no. 3 (1995): 159–65; Gloria Ladson-Billings, *The Dreamkeepers: Successful Teachers of African American Children* (San Francisco, CA: Jossey-Bass Inc., 1994); Django Paris and H. Samy Alim, *Culturally Sustaining Pedagogies: Teaching and Learning for Justice in a Changing World* (New York, NY: Teachers College Press, 2017).

2. "5 Keys to Rigorous Project-Based Learning," Edutopia, June 25, 2014, https://www.edutopia.org/; John Larmer, John R. Mergendoller, and Suzie Boss, *Setting the Standard for Project Based Learning: A Proven Approach to Rigorous Classroom Instruction* (Alexandria, VA: ASCD, 2015); Joseph L. Polman, Kristina Stamatis, Alison Boardman, and Antero Garcia, "Authentic to Whom and What? The Role of Authenticity in Project-Based Learning in English Language Arts," in *Rethinking Learning in the Digital Age: Making the Learning Sciences Count*, ed. Judy Kay and Rosemary Luckin, 13th International Conference of the Learning Sciences (ICLS) 2018, Volume 3 (London, UK: International Society of the Learning Sciences).

CHAPTER 4

1. Elizabeth G. Cohen, *Designing Groupwork: Strategies for the Heterogeneous Classroom*, 2nd ed. (New York, NY: Teachers College Press, 1994).

2. Cohen, *Designing Groupwork*, 164.

3. Rachel A. Lotan, "Group-Worthy Tasks," ASCD (Educational Leadership, March 2003), http://www.ascd.org/publications/educational_leadership/mar03/vol60/num06/Group-Worthy_Tasks.aspx.

4. Elizabeth G. Cohen, Rachel A. Lotan, Beth A. Scarloss, and Adele R. Arellano, "Equity in Cooperative Learning Classrooms," Equity in Cooperative Learning Classrooms | Complex Instruction, 0AD, https://complexinstruction.stanford.edu/about/Equity-in-Cooperative-Learning-Classrooms.

5. Cohen et al., "Equity in Cooperative Learning Classrooms."

CHAPTER 5

1. John Hattie and Helen Timperley, "The Power of Feedback," *Review of Educational Research* 77, no. 1 (March 2007): 81–112, https://doi.org/10.3102/003465430298487.
2. Grant Wiggins, "Seven Keys to Effective Feedback," *Educational Leadership* 70, no. 1 (September 2012): 10–16, http://www.ascd.org/publications/educational-leadership/sept12/vol70/num01/Seven-Keys-to-Effective-Feedback.aspx.
3. Wiggins, "Seven Keys to Effective Feedback," 10–16.
4. Hattie and Timperley, "The Power of Feedback," 81–112; Wiggins, "Seven Keys to Effective Feedback," 10–16.

CHAPTER 6

1. Sam Wineburg, *Historical Thinking and Other Unnatural Acts: Charting the Future of Teaching the Past (Critical Perspectives on the Past)* (Philadelphia, PA: Temple University Press, 2001).

CHAPTER 7

1. Karen Hammerness, *Seeing Through Teachers' Eyes: Professional Ideals and Classroom Practices* (New York, NY: Teachers College Press, 2006).
2. "Diana Laufenberg," Inquiry Schools, 2020, https://www.inquiryschools.org/diana-laufenberg.
3. "Core Practices—A Complete List with Links to Each Practice," EL Education, 2020, https://eleducation.org/resources/the-core-practices-a-complete-list-with-links.
4. "Redefining and Raising Student Achievement," EL Education, 2020, https://eleducation.org/who-we-are/our-approach.
5. "Major Study Shows: EL Education Literacy Partnerships Drive Higher Student Achievement," EL Education, 2020, https://eleducation.org/impact/curriculum/curriculum-research-studies/teacher-potential-project.
6. "EL Education Upcoming Events," EL Education, 2020, https://eleducation.org/news-and-events/calendar.
7. "Matthew Riggan," The Workshop School, 2020, http://workshopschool.org/

CHAPTER 8

1. Anna Saavedra et al., "Knowledge in Action Efficacy Study," (in press, 2017), https://sprocket.lucasedresearch.org/.
2. Jean Anyon, "Social Class and the Hidden Curriculum of Work," *Journal of Education* 162, no. 1 (1980): 67–92, https://doi.org/https://doi.org/10.1177/002205748016200106.
3. Paulo Freire, "Reading the World and Reading the Word: An Interview with Paulo Freire," *Language Arts* 62, no. 1 (January 1985): 15–21, https://doi.org/DOI: 10.2307/41405241, 15
4. Freire, "Reading the World," 15,
5. Freire, "Reading the World," 15–16.

ACKNOWLEDGMENTS

In so many ways, we have regarded this book as our own version of a long-term project, and as with any project, the success of the outcome depends on the quality of engagement and collaboration of those who are working on it. We have been blessed to have a team that has remained engaged and highly collaborative throughout the writing of this book, even through the challenges of a global pandemic and renewed efforts to work for racial justice. Book projects also benefit from feedback and iteration, and we want to thank our editor, Caroline Chauncey of Harvard Education Press, and the anonymous reviewers of the original prospectus for the excellent feedback they've provided. We also want to thank Caroline, editor par excellence, for all her encouragement around this work. We also want to thank Elizabeth Petela, who has supported this project all along the way with her careful copyediting, outstanding technical support, and good cheer.

We also want to thank all of our partners and the many teachers and leaders who helped design, contributed to, and participated in the University of Pennsylvania Project-Based Learning Certificate Program. We have an extraordinary groups of advisors, including Chris Lehmann of Science Leadership Academy; Matthew Riggan of the Workshop School; Meg Riordan, formerly of EL Education and now at The Possible Project; and Shaquita Smith of the School District of Philadelphia, who provided invaluable advice and feedback throughout the project and contributed to this work in meaningful ways. We have learned so much from them. The

Penn PBL team could not function without the intellectual, relational, organizational, and professional acumen of Sara Goldstein, Chenelle Boatswain, Liz Gotwalt, JeanMarie Farrow, Rachel Kuck, Jesslyn Poulson, Jiayue Gu, Diana Bowen, Radhika Kapoor, Adam Lang, Catherine Ward, and Betty Chandy. In addition, we have been extremely lucky to be supported by many brilliant thought partners over the years, including Emily Rainey, Annie Garrison Wilhelm, Mary Hauser, Preeti Samudra, Caitlin Thompson, Emily Shahan, Rachel Folger, Bobbi Kurshan, Janine Remillard, Lisette Enumah, Rachel Ebby-Rosin, Susanna Owens Farmer, Michael Golden, Benjamin Greenwald, Kimberly A. Johnson, Maria Morrison, Thomas Szczesny, and Kristin Hoins. We are eternally grateful for the insightful work of the PennPBL coaches, both past and present, who have taught within our Project-Based Learning Certificate Program, including Alissa Fong, Deb Morrison, Tina Schuster, Jordan Templeton, Tyler Thigpen, Richard Staniec, Melissa Viola-Askey, and Gina Wickstead. We would also like to thank the Lucas Education Research Foundation, and especially Kristin DeVivo, Nathan Warner, and Denis Udall for their belief in and support of this project over the past five years. We could not have written this book without their support.

Finally, we would like to thank all of the teachers who participated in the PennPBL research and University of Pennsylvania Project-Based Learning Certificate Program and those who helped us along the way. You have embraced the challenge of this work and inspired us all with your commitment to ensuring that all students have the opportunities to grow and learn through engaging in projects of their own. We dedicate this book to you with appreciation and deep respect.

ABOUT THE AUTHORS

PAM GROSSMAN is the dean and George and Diane Weiss Professor at the Graduate School of Education at the University of Pennsylvania and the Nomellini-Olivier Professor Emerita at the Stanford Graduate School of Education. She has published broadly in the areas of teacher education and professional education more broadly, teacher knowledge, and the teaching of English in secondary schools. Her most recent work focuses on practice-based teacher education. A former high school English teacher, Dr. Grossman is a long-time teacher educator. She holds a BA in English from Yale University, a master's in education from the University of California, Berkeley, and a PhD from Stanford. While at Stanford, she was the founding director of the Center to Support Excellence in Teaching and the founder of the Hollyhock Fellowship for early career teachers in underserved schools.

ZACHARY HERRMANN serves as the executive director of the Center for Professional Learning at the University of Pennsylvania Graduate School of Education (Penn GSE). Dr. Herrmann also serves on the professional faculty within the Teaching, Learning, and Leadership Division at Penn GSE, and as the academic director for the Project-Based Learning Certificate Program. Dr. Herrmann taught high school mathematics for several years, during which time he developed a collaborative professional development network of schools dedicated to improving teaching and learning with a focus on complex tasks, collaborative learning, and equity. He holds a BS in mathematics and a master's in educational administration and leadership from the University of Illinois, an MA in education from Stanford University, and a Doctor of Education Leadership from the Harvard Graduate School of Education.

SARAH SCHNEIDER KAVANAGH is an assistant professor at the Graduate School of Education at the University of Pennsylvania. Her research focuses on teacher education and professional development. In particular, she is interested in how teachers can be supported to instantiate their principles relating to justice and equity into their daily classroom practice. Dr. Kavanagh comes from a background as an English and history teacher in middle and high schools and holds a BA in American Studies from Wesleyan University and a PhD from the University of Washington. While at the University of Washington, she was the founding director of Teacher Education by Design and, since arriving at Penn GSE, she has worked closely with this team of authors to design, build, and study the Project-Based Learning Certificate Program.

CHRISTOPHER G. PUPIK DEAN is a senior fellow and the codirector of the Independent School Teaching Residency Program at the Graduate School of Education at the University of Pennsylvania. Dr. Pupik Dean's research interests focus on teacher education, citizenship education, and ethics. In addition to his work on teacher education for project-based learning, his current work focuses on the role of the humanities in human development. Dr. Pupik Dean earned his bachelor's degree in Education, Theory, and Policy from the Pennsylvania State University's Schreyer Honors College and his master's degree and PhD in Education, Culture, and Society from the University of Pennsylvania. Before enrolling at Penn GSE, Dr. Pupik Dean taught grades nine through twelve environmental science in Henderson and Durham, North Carolina.

INDEX